D1591212

*A Gothic Sermon*

AHMANSON · MURPHY
FINE ARTS IMPRINT

THE AHMANSON FOUNDATION

has endowed this imprint

to honor the memory of

FRANKLIN D. MURPHY

who for half a century

served arts and letters,

beauty and learning, in

equal measure by shaping

with a brilliant devotion

those institutions upon

which they rely.

# A Gothic Sermon

*Making a Contract with the Mother of God,*
*Saint Mary of Amiens*

Stephen Murray

UNIVERSITY OF CALIFORNIA PRESS

*Berkeley     Los Angeles     London*

BV
4243
.M87
2004

*The publisher gratefully acknowledges the
generous contribution to this book provided by
the Art Endowment Fund of the University of
California Press Associates, which is supported
by a major gift from the Ahmanson Foundation.*

University of California Press
Berkeley and Los Angeles, California

University of California Press, Ltd.
London, England

© 2004 by the Regents of the University of California

Library of Congress Cataloging-in-Publication Data

Murray, Stephen, 1945–
    A Gothic sermon : making a contract with the Mother
of God, Saint Mary of Amiens / Stephen Murray.
        p.    cm.
    "Sermon in honor of the Mother of God, Saint Mary
of Amiens" : P.
    Includes bibliographical references (p.      ).
    ISBN 0-520-23847-8 (cloth : alk. paper)
    1. Sermons, French.  2. Cathédrale d'Amiens.  I. Sermon
in honor of the Mother of God, Saint Mary of Amiens. English
and French (Old French)  II. Title.
BV4243.M87  2004
252'.02—dc22                                    2004009383

Manufactured in the United States of America

14  13  12  11  10  09  08  07  06  05
10  9  8  7  6  5  4  3  2  1

The paper used in this publication meets the minimum
requirements of ANSI/NISO Z39.48–1992 (R 1997) *(Permanence
of Paper).* ♾

*For my father, who preached many a memorable sermon*

# CONTENTS

# PLATES

# ACKNOWLEDGMENTS

I would like to thank the many colleagues who have helped me, especially Paul Papillo, Cecelia Gaposchkin, Richard Brilliant, David Nirenberg, and Georgia Wright. Phyllis Roberts and Elisabeth Brown have been generous with their encouragement and suggestions. Consuelo Dutschke kindly looked over my transcript, helping me to avoid many mistakes and to identify many of the preacher's quotations. Edward Markee smoothed many of the knots in my translation. Andrew Tallon undertook the photography. Although this is a project I began some years ago, much of the work was completed in 2000–2001, under the tenure of a fellowship at the Center for Advanced Study in the Behavioral Sciences at Stanford University. I wish to express my gratitude to the trustees and directors of the Center, especially Bob Scott. Kathleen Much provided invaluable editing help, and the work of my fellow Fellows invited me to consider the Gothic cathedral in relation to behavior modification. At the University of California Press, Rose Vekony provided final editing that was as inspired as it was rigorous. Finally, I thank the Trustees and Directors of the National Humanities Center, where I spent 2003–2004 as Henry Luce Senior Fellow during the last stages of production of this book.

A NOTE ON THE TEXT

For convenience of reading and reference I have introduced accents and punctuation where essential for meaning and have broken the text, somewhat arbitrarily, into numbered passages.

# Introduction

*A small congregation has gathered to listen to the visiting preacher.*
*We are in a church in or near Amiens, a city in Picardy where the*
*great Gothic cathedral of Notre-Dame, under construction for the past*
*half-century, is now substantially complete, the paint still fresh on the*
*sculptured portals. Our congregation is made up of country folk, some*
*of whom have substantial land holdings. It is morning.*

*The preacher addresses the members of his flock directly, in their*
*own language. It is as if he knows who they are, what they have been*
*doing, and the way they think. He ruefully pokes fun at himself. He*
*slyly mocks the established church. He pays equal attention to male*
*and female members of the congregation. Swearing profusely, he con-*
*demns such oaths, making his audience laugh. Yet, oddly enough, such*
*conduct only enhances the seriousness of his message. His vivid ver-*
*bal images and lively dialogue impart knowledge of the scriptures and*
*a sense of the apostolic mission, as he urges his listeners to enter into*
*a kind of contract with Saint Mary of Amiens — to buy into a coherent*
*strategy of salvation.*

. . .

More than twenty years ago, browsing in the printed catalogue of the collection of documents relating to Picardy (northeastern France) in the manuscript room of the Bibliothèque nationale, I came across an entry that promised the text of "a Picard sermon of the thirteenth century delivered, I believe, on the occasion of the construction of the cathedral of Amiens."[1] Thinking that the text might provide exciting information about the life of a medieval cathedral and how it was actually used by ordinary folk, as well as a better understanding of the phenomenon we call *Gothic*, I turned to the document itself, a small-format parchment codex from the Grenier Collection, written in a mid to late thirteenth-century hand that was fortunately quite legible. I read and began to transcribe, and as I continued to reflect on the piece in ensuing months and years, the scenario sketched above formed ever more clearly in my mind.

Before entertaining any such "certainties," however, let us first remind ourselves: *Ceci n'est pas un sermon;* this is not actually a sermon. A sermon, in order to be fully a sermon, must be performed and experienced.[2] What we have here is a written document. The text certainly implies an intention to preach, but it is impossible to prove that any such public oration took place, since we have no eyewitness accounts. The text may have remained a written composition intended for silent perusal.[3] Or perhaps a preacher had prepared it for future presentation; perhaps he or someone else transcribed it ex post facto.[4] The fact that the piece was written down suggests that it may have been considered a useful model—something that might be adapted for a number of different occasions.

The two eminent scholars of French medieval literature who have studied the text, Albert Lecoy de la Marche and Michel Zink, came away with very different conclusions, agreeing only on the obvious: that this is not a learned discourse intended for an educated audience.[5] The preacher does not take as his theme a single scriptural text and proceed to open its multiple levels of meaning: historical, allegorical, tropological, and anagogical. There are no clearly marked subdivisions and no linkage with any liturgical feast. Part of the preacher's agenda was certainly to raise funds for the Gothic cathedral of Notre-Dame of Amiens sometime around the main construction campaign—after the body of the edifice was complete, but as work continued on the upper west facade and the choir screen and was about to begin on the nave chapels.[6] Lecoy de la Marche, who in 1868 wrote one of the first great (and still useful) reference books on medieval preaching, concluded that the sermon was delivered in Amiens Cathedral by a member of the clergy, possibly a mendicant, who had been delegated by the bishop at a time when major construction was still underway, toward 1269. The congregation that presumably gathered in the space of the crossing and in the eastern bay of the nave would have been made up of the faithful from the immediately surrounding area.

It is quite tempting to associate the seductiveness of the preacher's rhetoric with the amazing spaces and forms of the Gothic cathedral of Notre-Dame of Amiens. The close relationship between the cathedral clergy and the mendicants (the latter being Dominicans and Franciscans) testifies to the importance assigned to preaching in this space. In the tympanum of the central portal of the west facade, Saint Francis of Assisi leads the elect to heaven in what is perhaps the first sculptured image of this saint. We might also remember the reputation of the dean, Jean d'Abbeville, known for his sermons on the Song of Songs.[7] The metaphor of "meltdown," used to convey the affective response of the lover to the best-beloved *(sponsus* and *sponsa)* in the Song, can be matched with the sense of astonished pleasure as the visitor—having ascended the steps to the west portals, with the entire expanse of the towering frontispiece reduced to the funnel-like compressive space of the portal and the restricted aperture of the door—finally bursts into sacred space.[8] Unlike that of other cathedrals, such as Notre-Dame of Paris, Chartres, and Reims, the passage into the nave at Amiens is not darkly encumbered with heavy tower-supporting piers. The visitor gains an immediate, awe-inspiring view of the nave as it extends in length, height, and breadth through a measured succession of bays down to the brilliantly lit choir.

We can, if we like, visualize our little congregation gathered in the central crossing in front of the choir screen from which sermons and readings were delivered.[9] There were no pews—the audience would have stood or possibly sat on movable chairs that might be borrowed or rented for the occasion. Here, at the very heart of the edifice, the regular succession of nave bays gives way to a dramatic explosion of space as bays become wider, permitting dramatic diagonal views. This is the area where construction of the cathedral began in 1220 and from which its geometric matrix was generated. Those assembled here might experience the totality of the cruciform light-filled spaces of nave, transept arms, and choir as a kind of revelation.

But despite the repeated references our preacher makes to Saint Mary of Amiens, a closer reading of the text permits multiple interpretations of the locus of the sermon, as well as of its intent. Zink argued that the text resulted from a fund-raising relic quest conducted not in the cathedral but in a rural church in the diocese and the vicinity of Amiens. Lecoy de la Marche had considered that with its exciting *mouvement,* its unexpectedness and the liveliness of its images drawn from life, the text was written in haste, seeming like a first draft with numerous repetitions and little intellectual unity.[10] By contrast, Zink pointed to a rigorous underlying structure of echoes and reprises, artfully crafted in relation to the psychology of the fund-raising task at hand.

Interestingly, neither scholar made any reference to the forms of the cathedral of Notre-Dame. A full exploration of the intention of the preacher and putative responses of his congregation should obviously draw on the principal source of programmatic motivational images available to the thirteenth-century people of Amiens and the surrounding area: the portals of the Gothic cathedral of Notre-Dame of Amiens.[11] The handwriting of our text suggests a date close to the completion of the sculpture and its painting, when local people were abuzz with excitement over this remarkable new addition to the visual environment. Might vivid visual memories of the cathedral possibly enjoyed by members of the audience have mediated the experience of the sermon? Conversely, might the preacher's words have rung in people's heads as they looked at the sculpture?[12] Here, again, we can animate the problem by juxtaposing two opposite assessments. Were the portals of Amiens Cathedral, indeed, as John Ruskin suggested, a kind of open book—a sermon—which ordinary people, with minimal instruction, could understand? Or rather, should we agree with Marcel Proust in seeing the sculpture as arcane hieroglyphs?[13]

Although *in* the city, the cathedral was not principally *of* the city; rather, it was the center of a rural diocese that was dotted with prosperous villages. The funds for cathedral construction were generated as much in the countryside as in the city. The ordinary Picard country folk addressed by the preacher would therefore have been an important audience for the cathedral. The parallel structures found in the rhetoric of the sermon and the disposition of images in the complex program of the western frontispiece of the cathedral may be keys to the experience of that audience.

Evidence relating to the agrarian history of the area is one avenue for understanding the country folk in the audience. But another is the sermon itself. For the preacher, in responding to the needs of his flock, has left the character of that audience imprinted on his text. Dean Jean d'Abbeville of Amiens, no doubt a very learned preacher, was considered boring by some. Henry of Ghent remarked that the dean's sermons interpreting the Gospels were so overlaid with verbiage and citations from the scriptures that the overall structure was quite impossible to remember.[14] Our preacher does not make the same mistake. He has clearly studied the members of his audience and found ways to engage their interest. His best strategy was to persuade them to follow him by being like them. Similarly, the experiments that produced at least three distinct modes of carving in the sculptural program of the portals may be explained in terms of critical response. In order to engage their audience, the carvers (imagiers) and their clerical patrons reached toward a demotic style of carving that can be compared with the rhetorical mode of the sermo humilis.

In addition to the exploration of these issues, my objective here is nothing more (nor less) than to provide the reader with the opportunity of reading the sermon in its entirety, both in its original Old French and in my own English translation.[15] It is not enough to quote a sentence here or there, or to attempt to crystallize, in a pithy epigram, a sermon that must have lasted for the better part of an hour. Just as students of the cathedral need access to the monument itself—to enter it, to explore its length, breadth, and height—so students of thirteenth-century religious life need to read the entire sermon, gauging its tone as well as its content, in order to reach their own conclusions.

I

# Occasions and Audience

With all the caveats expressed in the Introduction, let us nonetheless assume that there was an intention to compose or to preach a sermon, and perhaps also that the sermon was preached on at least one occasion and that it was heard and transcribed. The preacher addresses a small group of people gathered in a church in honor of the Mother of God, Saint Mary of Amiens (1). *Mary* can be understood in four ways: as a historic person, distant in time and place (the mother of Christ, or the "Mother of God": *Mère Dieu*); as an institution (mother church, which provides the sacraments); as a building (Notre-Dame, cathedral of Amiens, under construction at that time and in need of financial resources for completion); and as a most efficacious and ever-present patroness and champion who has a direct personal relationship with the repentant sinner. It is precisely the preacher's skillful play on this multivalent identity that provides the sermon with much of its subtle force.

From the very beginning of the oration the preacher emphasizes the power of the bishop (in place of Christ), and hence the authority of the episcopal demand that the arrival of the relics and the message of Notre-Dame of Amiens, as well as the celebrations associated with them, be treated with the same respect as that paid to Christmas, Easter, or Sunday.[1] Dire consequences are threatened for the disobedient priest who might fail to welcome the arrival of the bishop's ambassador and the relics: "Your lord the priest, has he obeyed my lord the bishop?" (1–7, esp. 5). The reference to "your lord priest and all the other priests who are in his diocese" (3) reveals more about the identity of members of the audience than about the place where they had assembled. These are clearly parishioners, either gathered in their own church, urban or rural, or (and this seems less likely) having come to Amiens from the surrounding area to listen to a sermon delivered in the cathedral, perhaps by a visiting mendicant preacher. Given the possibility of multiple performances based on our text, both interpretations might apply. In 1240, at a time of fiscal need, the relics of Honoratus, sainted bishop of Amiens, were carried through the surrounding countryside in a quest for funds; such a relic quest is depicted in the tympanum of the south transept portal.[2]

Clearly this sermon was delivered by a preacher with a special mission outside the cyclical demands of the liturgy. One can deduce from the sermon's opening passages that certain local priests did not welcome the arrival of questers carrying the cathedral reliquaries, and that their response was considered a challenge to the authority of the bishop and the principal church of the diocese, the cathedral of Notre-Dame of Amiens. There is ample evidence of anticlericalism in the area around Amiens in the middle decades of the thirteenth century.[3] This situation resulted in the appointment of a visiting preacher charged by the bishop to reassert the authority of the mother church. Zink expresses surprise at the fact that although such missions could not have been rare, this is the only surviving sermon that may have arisen from one.[4]

The preacher makes no less than four promises of reward to those who contribute alms to mother church (136, 220, 225, and 226)—although to call this a fund-raising sermon would impose a reductive stereotype that fails to acknowledge the full range of the preacher's agenda and the audience's potential responses. The appeal for financial help is artfully contrived, drawing on the ambiguity inherent in the four different meanings of "Saint Mary of Amiens."

A clue in our attempt to understand the problem of time and place is our preacher's exhortation that simply coming to church would yield forty days of pardon without one's giving a penny "for meeting the needs of the [church of the] sweet Mother of God, Saint Mary, that she [or it] be fulfilled [or completed]" (31). Given the multiple meanings associated with "Mother of God," the use of the word *aconsomée* was probably calculated to lead the audience to think not only of pleasing Mary and disposing her to benevolence but also of completing the construction of the physical fabric of the cathedral. This implicit association between the material and the abstract was, as will be seen, a critical part of the preacher's strategy throughout. The reference to "completion" was used by Lecoy de la Marche and early students of the sermon as a means of dating the sermon before 1269, when the axial window of the choir clerestory was installed and the building allegedly completed. But 1269 does not mark the completion of the cathedral at all. The nave roof dates to about 1300; the choir screen and the lateral chapels of the nave were added in the decades either side of 1300; and work continued on the west towers throughout the Middle Ages. And in any event, the sermon could have been delivered once or several times before it was written down, and it could have been repeated well after the text was committed to writing.

Several more appeals follow: "Know truly that to all the benefactors of the church my Lady, Saint Mary of Amiens, sends 140 days of true pardon to mitigate the vivid penance that you must do in the cruel fire of purgatory" (136). "My lord the bishop sends pardon and absolution from all these sins to all men and women who send their alms to the church of my Lady, Saint Mary of Amiens; and so they will leave today on this holy morning as free [of sin] as Saint Mary Magdalene when she went from the beautiful feet of our Lord. Now let us pray God and his sweet mother that you will worthily receive [this pardon]" (220). And again, "Pray to our Lord to grant true pardon to all those men and women who send their alms and their fine gifts to the church of Notre-Dame, Saint Mary of Amiens. Then, good gentlefolk, my lord the bishop sends you pardon and absolution for all the legal suits that have been wrongly brought against you. For the amount that you send to the church of my Lady, Saint Mary of Amiens, you shall be quit accordingly of the whole sum, the half or quarter" (225–26).

Yet despite the oft-repeated appeals for alms for the mother church, there is much more to this piece than fund-raising, as consideration of the entire performance and the broader issues will show.[5]

2

# Structure and Content

Unlike most thirteenth-century sermons, which feature a clear organizing matrix with well-defined subdivisions, this repetitive and rambling piece has no readily discernible structure. Whereas contemporary sermons would explore a particular biblical text at various levels—historical, allegorical, anagogical, and tropological—our preacher remains almost entirely on the tropological, or moralizing, level, citing only fragmentary texts from the scriptures with references (insouciant, at times) to the Fathers. His principal illustrations are vivid vignettes and exempla. His "demonstrations" are lively stories.

In a spectacular piece of revisionist scholarship, Michel Zink argued that the preacher's apparently artless flow of consciousness is deceptive—that the piece was, in fact, rigorously organized in two distinct parts, with a halfway turning point articulated through the almost verbatim repetition of the opening protocol.[1] Thus the preacher, having begun, "Good gentlefolk, as few of you as have gathered in the holy church in honor of the glorious Mother of God, Saint Mary of Amiens" (1), returns at the halfway point to a very similar formula: "Good gentlefolk, all of you together and each of you individually who recognize the Mother of God, Saint Mary of Amiens, which is your mother church" (134). Both at the beginning and at the midpoint the preacher emphasizes the power of the bishop of Amiens: in the first instance his authority over the local priest, and in the second his ability to lead the audience to paradise. For Zink this simple two-part structure facilitated a potent manipulative strategy, projecting theoretical considerations both to justify and to conceal the preacher's central agenda: the announcement of episcopal indulgences that would produce income.

Zink was certainly perceptive in recognizing this rhetorical bookmark at the middle of the sermon. But, in fact, the overlapping themes of the successive phases of the sermon obscure any tight structural organization—and given the repetition everywhere apparent in the piece, the presence of one more repeated formula might well have escaped an audience seduced by the word images, the reported dialogues, and the anecdotes of an amusing entertainer. The presumed intention may therefore have been quite different from the effect.

On reading the piece, one is tempted to divide it into overlapping clumps of related thoughts and to consider the dynamism of the transitions between them. Within any of the segments the preacher was likely to return to a theme already covered or to anticipate the next, all the while interspersing vignettes and exempla of such intensity that one quite forgets the overall train of thought—which is then reestablished by sheer repetition. Elements of a particular thought are thus placed in the mind well before the theme is actually developed. Verbal repetition—the address "good gentlefolk" *(bele douce gent)* is used about forty times—imparts a rhetorical unity to the whole.

As readers existing in a world beyond that of the preacher and his little congregation, we have the privilege of reaching our own conclusions about the central theme of the sermon and what it was intended to achieve in people's hearts and minds. For us, the piece can mean different things to different people.[2] Nonetheless, we must recognize that from the very start, the preacher insists on a causal relationship between disobedience, judgment, and damnation, passing quickly from disobedient priests to men and women who remain in a state of sin similar to Adam and Eve's. Those surprised by death and judgment in their fallen state are doomed to the agonies of hell. This premise, of course, forms the basis of many a sermon; Larissa Taylor put it most eloquently in *Soldiers of Christ:* "A pessimistic anthropology [i.e., human nature] was therefore balanced by an optimistic soteriology in which, thanks to God, everything was possible for the repentant sinner."[3]

Despite his gloomy premise, then, the preacher weaves together three powerful strategies open to the listener who wanted to escape the horrible certainty of hell by entering into a new contract. The first path of salvation comes with repentance and a life of good works. Second, we have the efficacy of the established church, with its abbots, bishops, priests, and sacraments. And finally, there is the benevolent agency of the Virgin Mary, who *is* the church. Each of the three paths can lead to pardon, or a release from the causal relationship between disobedience and damnation. As I suggest in chapter 4, these three paths are also evoked in the main portals on the west facade of Amiens Cathedral (plate 1). Entry to sacred space was provided by means of three parallel avenues of salvation that were, metaphorically, one and the same—just as the preacher argued that the power of the bishop to grant pardon (see the trumeau of the north portal; plate 8) was identical to that of the Virgin Mary (matching trumeau in the south portal; plate 11). But before looking further at the sculptural program, let us consider the sermon itself, in terms of both content and rhetorical strategy.

## 1. DISOBEDIENCE LEADS TO DAMNATION AT THE LAST JUDGMENT (1–24)

Having first situated the members of his audience and their priest in relation to the authority of the church of the Mother of God, Saint Mary of Amiens, and the power of its bishop, the preacher emphasizes the need for obedience. He informs the people that the bishop has ordered their priest and all the other priests of the diocese to respect the arrival of the relics and the word of the mother church (Notre-Dame of Amiens) as they do the feast days of Christmas and Easter. Priests must be obedient—the garb of the priest is itself a sign of obedience (see the images of bishops in the north portal, plates 6–8). The disobedient priest will be punished. Disobedience stems from original sin (the story of Adam and Eve is told in six sculptured images at the base of the trumeau of the south portal, plate 12). The rehearsal of the disobedience of Adam and Eve leads the preacher to an impassioned admonition on the final damnation that will result from disobedience (central tympanum, plate 5). "'Sinner,' said our Lord, 'there, where I find you, there I shall judge you.' Know, therefore, and doubt not, that the men and women who stayed away, as I said, will be taken in an evil hour. Know in good sooth that if they were taken on their land without having confessed their sins and repented, they would be condemned to death and suffer the pangs of hell; as God is God, he shall not spare them" (12).

Directly after this awful threat the preacher offers a glimpse of the promise of redemption through confession and good works: "The proof of a person's love is [found in] his works" (14). But the redemptive theme remains undeveloped as the preacher returns (16–17) to reflect on the dreadful fate of the men and women who "have stayed away," failing to respond to the call of the mother church. The words of the preacher amount to a malediction: "you should know without any doubt that they shall be so grievously cursed"—and there follows a sonorous list of all those who might be included in the curse (17).[4]

## 2. THE FIRST PATH OF SALVATION: COME TO CHURCH, SEEK PARDON, AND MEND YOUR WAYS (25–72)

Saying, "Now, good gentlefolk, . . . I will tell you what you will do for me" (25–26), the preacher marks a rhetorical transition, quickly reestablishing positive control of his flock's attention and reassuring them that the torments he has just described so vividly can be avoided through a little act of goodness rendered to Saint Mary. This is a most engaging passage, inviting members of the congregation into a kind of collusion with the preacher. They are deputized to go find their neighbors, not only insisting they come to church but also denouncing their sins, foretelling their punishment (27), and outlining the benefits of pardon and absolution in terms of specific reductions in the amount of time spent in purgatory.

The engagement is physical: each step helps counteract the

negative effect of sins that have been committed. In defining the passage to church as a pilgrimage rendered in the service and in fulfillment of the Mother of God, Saint Mary, the preacher is clearly inviting members of his audience to set out from their rural villages to visit the mother church of the diocese, Notre-Dame of Amiens. It is here that "fulfillment" may also imply the material completion of the Gothic cathedral. The fact that the sermon marks the beginning of the pilgrimage and not the end supports the notion of its use in churches a short distance away from the cathedral of Amiens rather than in the cathedral itself.

This physical act of coming to church is echoed in the preacher's invitation to the members of the audience to move forward, "draw closer to me," lending their eyes for seeing, their ears for hearing, and their hearts for remembering (37).[5] They are rewarded for their obedience by the funny story of a preacher who is as wildly impassioned as he is utterly forgettable (38).

Then follows a fuller development of the theme that had been briefly introduced in the first section above: redemption through good works. It does not matter how you began, says the preacher, but how you will finish: "The crown is given not for the starting but the persevering" (39). We catch a glimpse of the virtues and vices: "You should have humility as opposed to pride, sweetness and love as opposed to perfidy" (44). The low-relief images in the quatrefoils of the central portal of Amiens Cathedral provide a much fuller map of the virtues and vices (plates 3 and 4). The preacher invites us to contrast Judas Iscariot, who started well but finished badly, with Mary Magdalene, who started badly and ended well. This is an extended reflection, embroidered with many engaging embellishments and its own heading, "On Mary Magdalene."[6] In this way the preacher sets out to empower the individual, animated by the church, which is Saint Mary of Amiens, to redeem himself by changing his life in response to the prototypes offered.

### 3. THE SECOND PATH OF SALVATION: THE AGENCY OF THE MOTHER OF GOD, SAINT MARY OF AMIENS (73–87)

With a beautiful panegyric for the Mother of God, Saint Mary of Amiens, the preacher opens the second avenue of salvation (south portal). This Lady, the queen of heaven and the spouse of the Lord, intervenes for those who have fallen; she protects the weak and guards women. Sin came into the world through woman; it was defeated through woman. This discourse leads to Eve, the initiator of original sin; to the Virgin Mary as the new Eve; and to the story of Theophilus, which illustrates the potential of repentance and the power of the Virgin to break the contract with sin.[7] The emphasis on the ability of the Virgin (i.e., the church) to nullify a secular contract must have had particular resonance with members of the audience, all of whom labored under various kinds of contractual obligation, whether agrarian, communal, or commercial. The sermon develops this idea in subsequent passages.

### 4. THE POWER TO GRANT PARDON LINKS THE AGENCY OF THE VIRGIN MARY WITH THE AGENCY OF THE CHURCH (88–114)

Overlapping with and extending the illustration of the power of Mary to grant pardon to Theophilus is a lengthy discussion of confession and pardon. The preacher invokes Peter's denial and

Christ's forgiveness, the repentant Magdalene, the forgiven soldier who pierced Christ's side, and the thief who was crucified to the right of Christ. Those who fail to ask for pardon (Cain, Judas, the thief on Christ's left) do not receive it.

The calling of the apostles is treated at length (105–14) to show how human beings—ordinary folk, like the members of the congregation—gave up everything they had in order to achieve pardon. The two apostles paid for their pardon through martyrdom; such an illustration makes the pardon offered to the present congregation by the church seem an extraordinary bargain. This is emphasized by an account of the rigors of life in the various monastic orders (113)—all undertaken to achieve the pardon that here is offered at so little cost!

## 5. THE THIRD PATH OF SALVATION: THE CHURCH (115–33)

It is impossible to mark an exact transition from the treatment of pardon to the role of the historical and physical church. *Church* is projected, first, through the invocation of the presence of Saint Mary among those who have gathered on this holy morning (115). Members of the congregation have even greater need of the benefits that the Virgin Mary can provide than of the products of agrarian life: the land with its harvests of wheat and grapes (the quatrefoils in the north portal of the cathedral depict agrarian production; plates 6 and 7). *Church* is understood as the various people—starting with the apostles—who, for different reasons, bad as well as good, followed Christ during his lifetime (116–19). *Church* is invoked in Saint Peter's words to Christ and Christ's response: "Upon this rock . . ." (123). Peter was given the power to save and condemn on earth: this power descends to the pope, to archbishops, to bishops, and to priests—a most potent asset for a preacher charged by the bishop of Amiens to reimpose the authority of the mother church of the diocese, the cathedral of Notre-Dame (128). *Church* is also a physical entity made of stone (132). Having carefully and systematically established the basis of the power of the church to grant pardon, the preacher proceeds to make direct requests for money.

### 6. THE POWER OF THE CHURCH TO REDUCE THE SUFFERINGS OF PURGATORY AND LEAD YOU TO HEAVEN (134–68)

The repetition of the opening protocol here does, indeed, mark the halfway point, just as Zink has argued. But the transition to the more specific treatment of the power of the bishop of Amiens is blurred in a continuing elaboration of the theme of the benefits to be derived from the church/Saint Mary—namely, the sacraments: baptism, marriage, extreme unction, and burial (134).

*Church* is the power of the bishop to lead the elect to heaven together with the martyrs, confessors, and holy virgins (135). This heavenly company can be found in the archivolts of the central portal of the cathedral. It is through the church that one may reduce the pains of purgatory (vividly described in sections 138–42), both for oneself and for one's ancestors. The reduction of the days of suffering is clearly specified (136, 143, 148). The bishop and the church have ample power to extend pardon through the sacraments and offices (158). The church is established on local soil in the form of multiple institutions, all of which are working on the churchgoer's behalf (163–68).

As he describes the formidable salvific power of the church, the preacher intensifies the rhythm of his presentation with the drumbeat of a refrain repeated eight times, praying for a worthy reception of the pardon here offered (89, 115, 156, 159, 164, 166, 168, 220). And he now offers a reduction of the pain of purgatory in return for contributions to Our Lady, Saint Mary of Amiens.

## 7. THE PROMISE OF ABSOLUTION FROM OATHS (169–219)

At this point the preacher offers what might seem like an extraordinary promise to his listeners: the bishop "sends pardon and absolution for all the oaths *[seremens]* that you have ever sworn except two" (169). He cannot forgive those who have sworn to deprive somebody of their property or to attack the holy church. The bishop may be understood, then, as a type of Virgin Mary, with the power to issue pardon for those who, like Theophilus, have entered into a false oath or contract. The bishop also sends his pardon for those who have sinned with blasphemous oaths.

With intense reality the preacher illustrates how gratuitous blasphemy actually continues the bodily sufferings of Christ: "The butcher does not chop up the meat on his block more than you sinners tear the flesh of our Lord" (175). These thoughts lead our preacher to an extended vision of the physical sufferings of Christ—sufferings depicted not as something in the distant past but as ongoing and exacerbated by sinners, beginning with the Adam and Eve, whose original sin is recounted here for the second time (202–15). The loss incurred through original sin was redressed through the Virgin Mary in the Incarnation and Crucifixion of Christ.

From the preacher's emphatic admonitions one might conclude that gratuitous oaths made upon the crown of God, the wounds of God, the agony of God, and so on were exceedingly common among the thirteenth-century folk.[8] The intent was probably not just to engage the attention of members of the congregation and correct their failings but also to subtly undermine the validity and seriousness of any kind of oath. The preacher conflates two different meanings of *oath:* first, the formal declaration of a pledge or promise to meet an obligation of some kind, and second, the gratuitous or blasphemous invocation of the name of God or his attributes. There is, says the preacher, only one binding commitment—and that is to serve God: "Good gentlefolk, the apostle teaches us that nobody should agree to anything other than to serve God" (102).

## 8. THE REQUEST FOR FINANCIAL RECOMPENSE (220–27)

Having issued the elusive promise of pardon for false oaths, and building on the chain of "reasoning" and justification established in earlier passages, the preacher now asks for financial recompense. A promise of 140 days' remission from the pains of purgatory in return for gifts to the church of Saint Mary of Amiens had already been made halfway through the sermon (136). It is followed by two much more direct appeals: "My lord the bishop sends pardon and absolution from all these sins to all men and women who send their alms to the church of my Lady, Saint Mary of Amiens" (220). And again, "Pray to our Lord to grant true pardon to all those men and women who send their alms and their fine gifts to the church of Notre-Dame, Saint Mary of Amiens" (225).

The justification for such requests is, within the preacher's logic, compelling; it lies in questioning the conventional framework of possession based on contracts and promises. The bishop exercises the power to break promises or undertakings *(fiances)* that have been foolishly entered into (221, 224). These words will remind the listener that the bishop is a type of Virgin Mary, and that the Virgin had delivered Theophilus by annulling his pact with the devil. Release from such contracts may be obtained inasmuch as one has contributed alms to Saint Mary of Amiens (226). Since the power of earthly contracts has been challenged, all income and material possessions come into question. It is surely better to give up doubtful possessions than to risk being caught with them at judgment time. *Rendre ou pendre:* give it back or hang (172, 227).

## 9. EPILOGUE: WHAT DO YOU ACTUALLY OWN? BETTER TO GIVE IT AWAY THAN RISK FINAL DAMNATION (228–52)

That we should not retain possession of wealth or goods that have been acquired under questionable circumstances is vividly illustrated in the final exemplum. In a sermon within a sermon, the preacher refers to a story he had heard preached in Abbeville (north of Amiens) by Friar Wedoir of Saint-Riquier. A townsman had found a considerable sum of gold inadvertently left behind by a merchant who had lingered in prayer before an image of Saint Mary in a church in a fine city like Amiens or Paris. Rather than keep this accidentally-acquired wealth, the townsman found an ingenious way of returning it.[9] The merchant, overwhelmed by this honesty and good-heartedness, did not want to accept the return of his own money and ran off. The townsman then accused him of robbery—of attempting to steal his honesty and reputation by leaving him in possession of wrongly-acquired goods. The audience surely found this tale compelling, first seduced by the dream of sudden acquisition of vast wealth (akin to today's Lotto) and then startled by the idea that a man could lose his virtue by allowing himself to be left with a possession that was not rightfully his.

Although our manuscript breaks off here, it is not difficult to extend this train of thought and reach the sermon's conclusion. We have been led step by step to question all earthly situations and contracts, as well as the ways in which possessions and wealth have been acquired. There is far more to be gained from the pardons extended by Saint Mary, who is at once the Virgin and the church—and by the bishop, whose authority parallels hers—than from the retention of wealth that is not rightfully ours. It seems particularly significant that the wealth was in the hands of a merchant returning from a fair; the country folk in the audience might have agreed that the generation of such wealth was indeed highly questionable.[10]

The recounting of this lively story provides our transition from the treatment of the admittedly soft-edged structure of the sermon to the rhetorical style and the sharply-painted vignettes that were intended to make it memorable.

# 3

# Rhetorical Strategies

## *The Art of Persuasion*

Our sermon comes alive when read aloud. Of course, it is impossible to be certain about the correspondence of our text with the putative performance, and we can never recover the effects of the preacher's cadences, pauses, gestures, grimaces, winks, or special emphasis on a word or syllable. One wonders, for example, how much the preacher played on the relationship between *pardonner* and *par donner:* you may have pardon by giving.[1] The rhyming *rendre ou pendre* (172 and 227) would, no doubt, have tripped off his tongue with particular force.

The preacher resorts to several different strategies to secure the attention of his congregation.[2] He addresses them directly and repeatedly with a range of assiduously polite greetings: "good gentlefolk" *(bele douce gent),* "good people" *(bele gent),* "good friend" *(biaus amis),* "my friends, men and women, my sons, my daughters" *(mi ami, mes amies, mi fil, mes files).* One remark singles out the women *(dame),* and he uses second-person to address a specific couple: "Good friend, and you, good lady friend" *(biaus amis et tu, bele amie).* Such greetings occur about fifty times—perhaps once a minute on average, and sometimes more frequently.[3] One imagines the amusement of members of the audience at the attention paid to a particular couple in his congregation.[4] One imagines the satisfaction on the part of the rural folk (would they have looked a little like Brueghel's peasants?) at this excessively polite form of address delivered so many times. This is not necessarily the kind of language they would routinely hear from members of the higher clergy of the cathedral or from the wealthier townsfolk of Amiens. In this way the preacher establishes a collusive relationship with his audience.

Within the text we find more than thirty fragments of Latin; these are summarized in the appendix. The extracts are mostly derived from the scriptures, with a preference for Matthew's Gospel. They are written in a bolder hand, and the initial capital letter carries a flourish. Most of the texts correspond closely to the Vulgate; others, however, particularly the ones ascribed to the Fathers (Gregory and Augustine), seem garbled. Such mixtures are common in sermons and liturgy, giving us a text that is *farci* (sometimes called *macaronic,* in cases where Latin is the dominant language).[5] Zink points out that the scriptural text that provided the theme of a vernacular sermon was commonly rendered in Latin, allowing the preacher to express respect for the language of the church. The practice also lent the speaker the aura of a learned person—one whose head was so full of the scriptures and the Fathers that bits seemed to spill out almost involuntarily. We might recall the words of Chaucer's Pardoner, "I speak some words in Latin—just a few—to put a saffron tinge upon my preaching and stir devotion with a spice of teaching."[6] The preacher might hope that members of his audience would actually retain some of his catchier jingles; "Ubi te invenero, ibi te iudicabo" is particularly memorable.

Our preacher seems at times to be engaged in parody. As part of his program of collusion, he gently mocks his ecclesiastical colleagues with facetious references to this or that figure of authority and the gratuitous parsing of a biblical phrase (6, from 1 Samuel 15:22).[7] In regard to the orders of the church, established through its institutions, offices, and sacraments, the preacher adopts an ambiguous stance. On the one hand, he respects the church as a powerful salvific machine working on behalf of the repentant sinner. On the other, he clearly anticipates a certain level of anticlericalism on the part of his lay audience, and he carefully indicates his sympathy. He asks his congregation, "Your lord the priest, has he obeyed my lord the bishop?" (5). Although he quickly responds in the affirmative, the fact that he would even pose such a question might have caused a *frisson*. He later makes scathing reference to all the purchasing done by the well-established orders of the Premonstratensians, Benedictines, Augustinians, and Cistercians (112). However, he is careful not to push the anticlerical sentiment too far.

The most dramatic illustration of the preacher's paradoxically contradictory stance is his approach to oaths and swearing. In condemning the gratuitous use of oaths, he himself swears repeatedly, "May God help me!" Such expletives form an essential part of the repetitive rhetorical fabric of the sermon.[8] His repeated use of *Dex* for Dieu and the many curses he cites, such as "by the eyes of Dog!" (*par les ex bieu!* [103]), were no doubt intended to reveal that he was essentially like the ordinary folk in his congregation.

Our preacher affects an engaging self-consciousness about his own role in relation to the audience, occasionally poking fun at himself. For example, in his opening words he reverses the expected formula, "To you, as *many* as are gathered here . . . ," ruefully addressing his remarks to as *few* as are gathered *(tant poi de vous)*. Surprised, members of the audience might look around to take stock of the fullness or emptiness of the space, even counting the numbers of the assembled flock. (Given the possible irony of these words, they may tell us nothing about the actual size of the audience.)

The construction of sermons within the sermon also underlines the preacher's self-conscious stance. Chapter 2 describes the embedded tale of the merchant's lost gold, first told by Friar Wedoir of Saint-Riquier, with which the manuscript ends. In an earlier story the preacher demands the total attention of the audience, insisting they physically approach: "Draw closer to me, and lend me your eyes for seeing and your ears for hearing and your hearts for remembering" (37). He then proceeds to tell of an impassioned preacher—one who is *passionné* rather than *passionnant*—who rants and raves but leaves no clear recollection of what he has said. One imagines members of the audience turning to each other in laughing recognition of the shared experience, and rewarding with their attention—for a while at least—this preacher who is not boring like the others. Teachers of all kinds will be familiar with this trick.[9]

With this strategy of lively engagement comes the preacher's ability to invoke the immediacy of his audience's physical presence in time and space, as well as their arrival in the building. Here is the place where salvation is made available; out there in the fields one risks being taken in a state of sin. He invokes the real presence of Saint Mary of Amiens among his congregation:

"Good gentlefolk, the Mother of God, Saint Mary, has called for your help on this holy morning, not because she needs you but because of the great need you have of her" (115). This need is compared to the need for material sustenance—food and drink. Similarly, the physicality of the church is invoked with a vivid image of the devil's discomfort on the day that the first squared stone of the building was laid. In the cathedral as well, the idea of the presence of Saint Mary of Amiens is translated into the material world through images like the trumeau figure of the south portal, the *Mère Dieu* (plate 11), and the *Vierge dorée* of the south transept portal (plates 14–15).

An emphasis on things material—presumably geared to the mentality of the audience—recurs throughout. For example, the continuing physical results of each individual's sins on the body of Christ and on his or her own ancestors is repeatedly stressed: "Good gentlefolk, in these great torments that I have described are the souls of your fathers and your mothers, the souls of your sisters and your brothers, the souls of your friends, men and women, who today are praying to you for pity; do you know what they are saying? 'Have pity on me, have pity on me, at least you my friends, because the hand of the Lord hath touched me'" (152).[10] "Bad Christians, men or women, who neither love God nor believe in him are worse than the tyrants who beat God at the whipping post or those who crucified him. . . . They blocked up their noses and ears, because it seemed to them that the word of our Lord and his blessed precious flesh stank" (16).

It is in this world of pressing physical needs and vivid experiences that the preacher exhorts his listeners to apply all their sensory and corporeal faculties to the task at hand. The first step is to direct their bodies (and those of their neighbors) to church—

*venés au moustier!* This in itself, however, is not enough: they must also be aware of the risk involved in remaining in the place of sin (27). The experience of attending the church is both somatic and kinetic—one has to move. Conversion is also understood in somatic terms; thus, when Theophilus heard the offices of the Virgin and turned away from sin, his conversion was not purely cerebral or spiritual; rather, "his blood was moved and his heart was turned" (84).

The visual images drawn by the preacher include a couple of direct references to the world of art. Referring to the need for awareness of sin, the preacher reflects that "the painter whitens the image that he paints just as much as you whiten your sins" (97). More vivid is the exhortation to paint a mental picture of purgatory with its cruel fires of red and green (141).

The audience would have been amused at the repeated use of sonorous lists, especially of the orders of the church: "There will be no archbishop, bishop, hermit, recluse, prior, abbot, priest, curate, chaplain, Dominican or Franciscan, white or black or gray monk, deacon or subdeacon, white or black nun, or cardinal of Rome . . . who would not be cursed" (17). The rhythmic, almost hypnotic power of these lists echoes that of Old Testament catalogs.

Fully aware of his audience's limited attention span and ability to resist his techniques—or perhaps not even notice them—the preacher strove to draw on common memories and experiences. The multisensory images he invoked might interact with other devotional lessons, both oral and visual. Perhaps the most powerful tool at the preacher's disposal was his ability to make people laugh.

The rhetorical characteristics defined above allow us to associate this text with the tradition of the *sermo humilis*.[11] Developed in the Gospels, this demotic, anticlassical language depends on direct interactions often conveyed through reported dialogue. Rather than seeking surface reality, this rhetorical mode uses underlying meanings brought out through typological linkages (the Virgin Mary with the bishop, for example). It is through such *figurae* and through simple words that we can reach the sublime. Wolfgang Kemp has explored the power of this mode of thought in popular preaching in the decades after 1200 and the potential links between sermons and the figurative programs of a cathedral (in this case, through its stained glass).[12] In a similar vein, we turn to the linkages between our sermon and the figurative program as seen in the portals of the Gothic cathedral of Notre-Dame of Amiens.

4

# Portals and Preaching

## *Image and Word*

As modern viewers, we really do not know how to look at the multiple elements of a Gothic sculptural program, which impose a massive image overload. Certainly, then, we have no idea how medieval people might have responded.[1] Now eroded, damaged, and stripped of polychromy, the sculptured images look dead—like fossils for us to arrange in "scientific" taxonomies. Recent conservation work has uncovered traces of the original paint applied to the sculpture at Amiens.[2] The column figures on the portals of the west facade, rendered only slightly larger than human scale in brightly colored, three-dimensional forms, might have once seemed uncanny in their closeness to real life—a kind of medieval "virtual reality."

It is all too easy for us to slip into the well-established habit of describing each portal as a unity, cataloging each element and relating it to visual or iconographic sources.[3] Modern scholars have found formal prototypes for each column figure and each sculptured element from the tympana and voussoirs. They have as-

33

signed a name to each portal—the portal of Saint Firmin (left, or north), that of the Virgin Mary (right, or south), and that of the Last Judgment (center)—placing it in stylistic, iconographic, and chronological relation to portals with similar themes and similar styles. Yet the habit of analyzing and classifying is an acquired one; there is no reason to believe that people in the Middle Ages looked or thought in this way. The ability to recognize a scene such as the Annunciation or the story of the invention of the relics of the local saint presupposes prior knowledge acquired through oral or written communication.[4]

One wonders how the "showing and telling" on the part of teachers and cathedral guides (like Malcolm Miller of Chartres) might have been practiced in the Middle Ages. Responses to the rhetorical strategies employed by the preacher to engage his audience's attention might well have been matched in the responses of ordinary folk to the sculpture. They might have seen themselves in the images of rural life and local people carved in the quatrefoils and tympanum of the left portal; they might have chuckled at the amusing carnal images crouching in the consoles of the solemn column figures.

Memory operates differently in relation to patterns of thought enunciated through the spoken word and those enunciated through images. In the former, although the speaker may insert occasional rhetorical markers to remind the listener of what has already been said or to anticipate what is to come, it is impossible to hear and comprehend the two narratives at the same time. The various elements of a sculptural program, however, can be seen simultaneously, or nearly so. From a short distance all three portals may be seen at the same time (plate 1), and even when a viewer examines this portal or that tympanum, he or she may easily refer to the other parts of the program or keep them in mind.[5]

The architectural framework of the facade sets up its own rigorous system of visual cross-reference. One quickly perceives the formal links between the trumeaux and tympana of the lateral portals (plate 1); it therefore comes as no surprise when the preacher portrays the bishop as a type of Virgin Mary, able to release the sinner from the consequences of his sin just as Mary did for Theophilus. In a similar vein, Wolfgang Kemp has explored the potential relation between sermons and the figurative program of a cathedral.[6] His study on the intertextuality of glass and sermon sheds important new light on how medieval people looked at images. His interest, however, is principally in formal parallels, such as that between clusters of images framed by the decorative armatures of the Prodigal Son window at Chartres, for example, and the divisions articulating a thirteenth-century sermon. More than in formal links, I am concerned with the underlying soteriological themes of sermon and sculpture—in how the complex program of the portals conveyed a coherent and unified message of salvation that matches, in some ways, the lessons of the sermon.

Of vital interest is the sermon's possible role in transmitting a program clearly devised by learned theologians to audiences made up largely of more or less uneducated people from the smaller towns and villages of the diocese of Amiens—the *rustici*. The portals of the cathedral convey a compelling program of salvation history—one in which the contract between God and his chosen people (the ark of the covenant, in the north portal, plate 13) has been superseded by a new contract through the Incarnation of Christ.[7] A connective tissue is provided by the screen of twelve minor prophets overlaid on the front surfaces of the four buttresses leading to the four great prophets on the inner surfaces of the buttresses flanking the central portal (plates 1–3). These are the preachers who belonged to the old order, and yet their vivid visions predicted and determined the new.[8] The prophecies of each individual—obscure at times—are illustrated in the quatrefoils below, like scholarly footnotes. In a sense, the lively vignettes framed in the quatrefoils allow the silent figures of the prophets to speak.[9]

Seen from a distance, the prophets on the buttresses and the column figures of the portals project an overwhelming degree of sameness (plate 1). In their search for appropriate figural form, the carvers generally eschewed a curved or contrapposto stance and complicated drapery; the figures stand foursquare, with equal weight on each foot and drapery falling, for the most part, in broad vertical folds. They belong to an ideal community: the church both militant and triumphant. These larger than life-size figures may have seemed to embody the perfection of the resurrected elect after the Second Coming, yet in their corporeality and with their painted faces they came alive in the time and space of the cathedral. The upright stance of each figure, signifying a human who has constructed himself in the likeness of Christ (plates 2–4), projects a rigidity and asceticism that is enhanced by contrast with the sensuous curves of the stocky carnal figure crouching in the supporting console.[10]

Those who responded to the preacher's command to "come to church" would encounter this ideal company at first from a distance. Continuing forward across the little square in front of the facade, such pilgrims would mount the steps to enter one of the three portals. Their very movement would recreate the passage of time as the line of Old Testament prophets culminated in Daniel, Ezekiel, Isaiah, and Jeremiah, who flank the central portal and then give way to the New Testament saints and apostles. In each portal the visitor would encounter interactive image clusters, the visual equivalents to the overlapping clumps of thought encountered in the sermon. Thus, one could approach the ranks of the apostles (plates 2–4) who line the central portal and encounter Christ the *Beau Dieu* and Christ the Judge (plate 5). One could turn to the agency of the legendary third-century(?) martyr and founder of the church in Amiens, Saint Firmin, and join the saints who line the embrasures of the north portal (plates 6–7). Or one could participate in the drama of the Incarnation, standing before the thaumaturgic Saint Mary of Amiens with the infant Christ, set upon the trumeau of the south portal (plate 11).

### 1. CENTRAL PORTAL: JUDGMENT AND REDEMPTION THROUGH TRANSFORMATIVE EMULATION (PLATES 1–5)

Although passage through the great central door would be reserved for special people (bishop and king) and for special days (Easter, royal entrances), there is no reason to believe that ordinary folk were denied access to the funnel-like, compressive space of the portal. There they could gaze up at the serried ranks of the apostles lining the embrasures and long to join them; study the low-relief sculptured images of the virtues and vices framed in quatrefoils in the embrasures (plates 3–4); stand at the foot of the central image of Christ, the *Beau Dieu;* and look up in awe at the events depicted in the lintel and tympanum (plate 5): the resurrection of the body, Saint Michael weighing bodies in the scales (lower lintel), the division of the saved and damned (upper lintel), and Christ the Judge flanked by the Virgin Mary and John (tympanum). In the voussoirs arching overhead are the orders of heaven: Old Testament patriarchs; the ancestors of Christ in a Jesse tree; virgins, confessors, martyrs, and angels.

If the members of our little congregation had indeed lent their eyes for seeing, their ears for hearing, and their hearts for remembering, they would have had no difficulty in applying the lessons of the sermon to the experience of the central portal.[11] The tropological program was clearly carried over from word to image, although not, of course, in a literal and direct fashion. Thus, the experience of the sculpture inverts the sequence of the preacher's message, which had begun with the terrible warning of the inescapable causal relationship between disobedience and hell and only later provided the elements of a strategy of salvation and the imitation of the apostles. In the upper lintel the jaws of hell seem distant, rather small, and not particularly threatening (plate 5). In medieval art we rarely encounter the devil, but instead we meet little demons who, in this case, appear as long-armed hairy beasties. Perhaps it is a question of scale, but the fellow who reaches out from the jaws of hell to grasp the leading sinner is hardly a menacing apparition. Are we supposed to chuckle at such narrative detail? Was it even possible for the image maker, or *imagier,* to match the horror of the preacher's words of malediction or his anticipation of the agonies of purgatory? Perhaps there is an element of sadistic pleasure as we follow the elaboration of the tortures to be suffered by the damned in the lower voussoirs on the right. This area is assumed to be purgatory, but it might also be seen as hell, since it is balanced by heaven on the other side.

Similarly distant is the powerful central image in the tympanum of Christ, who in the sermon continues to suffer as a result
of each person's sins (plate 5). The painted pupils of Christ's wide-
open eyes lend his gaze a hypnotic quality, as if he can see through
to the soul. From the ground, the apocalyptic image of Christ with
two swords issuing from his mouth, at the very tip of the tympanum, is barely visible.[12]

Much more immediate is the interaction between the visitor
and the apostles (plates 2–4). Just like the members of the congregation, these were ordinary folk who had been called by
Christ and built their lives on the prototype of Christ's life—in
the preacher's words, purchasing pardon for their sins through
martyrdom. The overwhelming sameness of the figures provides
a direct index of the fact that these are individuals who, in following the example of Christ, have formed themselves according to a single central template, here presented as the central
trumeau figure of the *Beau Dieu* (plate 2).[13]

The portal provides a chance for the viewer to redeem himself in a way much less demanding than the suffering of the apostles. The preacher has emphasized what a bargain this is—you
do not have to be crucified upside down like Saint Peter, but you
can achieve pardon by changing the path of your life: abandon-
ing sin and following the path of the virtues so clearly laid out in
the embrasures of the central portal (plates 3–4).

The sculptured images are, then, not passive objects intended
to evoke a purely aesthetic response on the part of the viewer.
Rather, in modeling himself on the image of the apostles, the
viewer might, in projecting himself (or his attention) forward,
find his prototype. The sermon allows us to understand the images of the apostles and of the virtues and vices in the quatrefoils

below them as interactive tools—both individually and as part of an entire program. The intention was clearly to provide the user with a powerful mechanism of change (you do not have to end as you began) leading to final triumph over sin. The portal and the sermon both provide multiple illustrations of such action, as well as exhortations to avoid vice and follow virtue. The presence of Saint Francis of Assisi at the head of the procession of the elect in the sculptured images to the left of the upper lintel emphasizes the key role that preaching played in the strategy of salvation.[14]

One who had listened attentively to our sermon, then, would bring to the central portal much of the understanding needed to make use of this tropological interactive program. The learned program encoded in the sculptured images was entirely in accord with what might have been the popular reading of them, sketched above. As Wilhelm Schlink has explained it, the central axis of the sculptural ensemble, with its triple images of Christ (the *Beau Dieu* of the trumeau, Christ the Judge in the tympanum, and the apocalyptic Christ at the summit), provided the exegetical fulcrum for the entire program.[15] Particularly important was the relation between the images derived from Psalm 90:13 (the triumph over the asp and the basilisk, seen in the central trumeau at the feet of Christ) and the Matthew 4 account of the temptation of Christ (plate 2). In the temptation the devil quotes the words of the Psalm, "If thou be the Son of God, cast thyself down, for it is written: That he hath given his angels charge over thee, and in their hands shall they bear thee up, lest perhaps thou dash thy foot against a stone" (Matt. 4:6; cf. Ps. 90:11–12). The point of the connection, according to Schlink, was to demonstrate that Christ, as a human being, was able to put the devil behind him. The central trumeau is thus an object lesson. If Christ, a human being, can triumph over sin, then so can you.

## 2. NORTH PORTAL: THE POWER OF THE CHURCH
### (PLATES 6–8)

The sculptural program asserts the notion of *church* on many levels. At the most visceral, the ranks of column figures at the base of the west facade show us the church as the assembly of the elect: the physical envelope of the church appears to be built on the prophets, the apostles, and the saints (plate 1).[16] The designers of the portal program, however, were at pains to construct the case that the Old Testament anticipated the New not only in the prophecy of the Incarnation of Christ but also in the forms and practices of the Christian church (including priesthood, with its external trappings), which they trace back to Moses, Aaron, and the patriarchs. Thus, turning from right to left, the viewer sees the six patriarchs depicted in the lower lintel of the south portal (the portal of the Virgin Mary, plate 13) become, in effect, the six bishops that occupy the same space in the north portal (plate 8); the Ark of the Covenant becomes the reliquary box containing the remains of the founding bishop, Saint Firmin; a new contract is formed through the very fact of Incarnation. This magic is worked through the persistence of vision. Furthermore, the repetitive mechanism that links the two lateral portals is a visual analog to the preacher's repeated insistence that Saint Mary of Amiens, the Mother of God, is indeed the church.

Like the sermon, the sculptural program makes a strong appeal to the ordinary folk of Amiens. It deliberately incorporates local lore—the story of the miracle associated with the relics of the founding bishop is told in the tympanum of the north portal (plate 8), while in the embrasures the bishops, saints, and martyrs of the diocese present themselves to the visitor (plates 6–7). Stylistically, too, the robust and round-faced figures in the tympanum and lintels are not the type of sculpture intended to appeal primarily to the educated.[17]

Although the performance of a sermon is diachronic, the repetitions in this sermon create powerful internal resonances that permit synchronic linkages, much as the sculptural program does. Thus, the preacher opens by identifying the power of the bishop with that of Christ—"Good gentlefolk, my lord the bishop of Amiens, who is our spiritual lord in place of our Lord on earth" (3)—emphasizing the hierarchy of subordination that bound the 777 parish priests of the diocese in obedience to the bishop. As discussed in chapter 2, this formula is repeated at the midpoint of the sermon with a direct enticement for the audience—the promise of heaven to those who would follow the bishop: "Our spiritual father, the lord bishop of Amiens, is duty-bound to conduct and lead you to paradise in the blessed company of angels, archangels, martyrs, confessors, and good and blessed virgins who have earned the kingdom of heaven through martyrdom and the shedding of their blood" (135).

This verbal image of the bishop is matched by the experience of the person who enters the north portal, drawn by the prototypical bishop, as a type of Christ, in the trumeau (plate 8), and then finds himself in the company of the saints, bishops, martyrs, and local virgin saint that line the portal jambs on either side (plates 6–7).[18] Gurevich has pointed to the power of the image of the saint in forging a link between the desires of the folk who used the portal and the clergy who commissioned it.[19] The latter wanted an instrument to impose conformity: a prototype to which ordinary folk could aspire. The people themselves wanted engaging stories tied to local soil, and above all, they wanted miracles. Both are available in the sculptured program of the north portal.

The central miracle of the diocese of Amiens is told in the tympanum directly above the trumeau image of the bishop (plate 8). The relics of the evangelist who had brought Christianity to the region having been lost, Bishop Sauve sought divine help to relocate them. A ray of light led him to the spot to dig, and there he found the relics miraculously preserved (center of upper lintel). The discovery caused a cold winter's day to become like summer: trees put out leaves and flowers bloomed. "The substance of all the elements was changed, and such a boiling heat came into the world that all the people present, in a state of ecstasy, were amazed."[20] Men, women, and children came from the neighboring cities—Thérouanne, Noyon, Cambrai, and Beauvais—to witness the miracle, and the sick were cured. The procession back to Amiens with the relics is described in terms reminiscent of Christ's triumphal entry into Jerusalem, with children climbing trees, foliage thrown into the road, and cries of "Hosanna!" (tympanum).[21] The image of the relic box would have resonated with the viewer's experience of relic processions and châsses in the surrounding villages (lower lintel). The miracle of the leaves and flowers was celebrated annually in the liturgy of *l'homme vert*. Into the cathedral every January 12 (the date Saint Firmin's relics were discovered) would come the Green Man, dressed in green and bearing foliage crowns for the clergy. The Green Man, seen on the extreme left following the relic procession in the tympanum of the portal of Saint Firmin, is depicted as a young man wearing a foliate crown; he has removed his overcoat because of the boiling heat.

That such local stories are absent from the sermon may lend credence to Lecoy de la Marche's suggestion that the preacher did not come from Amiens. He clearly did not think his audience needed him to talk about the life of Saint Firmin, focusing instead on saints who enjoyed a generic or universal character. He promises paradise through the personnel, institutions, and sacraments that the church has to offer rather than the local saints.

Indeed, the attempt to create a cult around the saints of Amiens was in some ways a failure. Today the identity of most of the ones portrayed on the north portal has barely survived in local memory. The exception is the image of the virgin saint, Ulphe (plate 6, the sixth figure from the door). Ulphe certainly achieved a following in the Middle Ages; her shrine was placed in the north choir aisle.[22] But what is known of Saints Ache and Acheul, the decapitated and head-bearing saints *(cephalophores)* who accompany Ulphe (third and fourth from the door)? An image of a bishop on the left has traditionally been seen as Honoratus, and two bishops on the right are possibly Firmin the Confessor and Saint Sauve (plate 7, first and third from the door). The figure identified in secondary sources as Saint Domice (second from the door), the companion and spiritual adviser of Saint Ulphe, is unforgettable for its realistic appearance, but the identity of the remaining three saints on the right (Gentien, Fuscien, and Victoric?) remains vague. Their portrayal suggests prophets more than saints.[23]

The most likely candidate for popular enthusiasm in the local college of saints was Bishop Honoratus, who was to receive his own portal in the south transept facade (plate 14). But Honoratus, the patron saint of bakers, could not withstand the force of the Virgin Mary. The place reserved for him on the trumeau of the south transept portal was in fact taken by Mary, in the form of the famous image of the *Vierge dorée,* carved and installed on the transept portal at a date very close to the handwriting of our sermon (plates 14 and 15). What did the Virgin Mary have to offer that was so compelling? The preacher gives the answer.

### 3. SOUTH PORTAL: THE *MÈRE DIEU* (PLATES 9–13)

In the south portal the designers of the sculptural program combined lofty images of the Dormition and Assumption, showing the Virgin Mary uncorrupted by physical decay after death and reigning at the right side of Christ in heaven (upper lintel and tympanum, plate 13),[24] with the earthly events of the Incarnation (column figures, plates 9 and 10). The quatrefoils depict the stories of Solomon and Sheba and of Herod (left, plate 9) opposite the story of John the Baptist and an elaboration of the theme of virgin birth (right, plate 10).

The life-size images of the Annunciation, Visitation, and presentation in the temple, as well as the three magi presenting their gifts across the space of the portal, invite the user to participate physically in the drama of the Incarnation (plates 9–10).[25] The preacher describes the Incarnation as the antidote to original sin: "Good gentlefolk, when our Lord saw that all was lost by the fault of a man, whom he had made . . . , he saw that just as everything had been lost by a man who was not conceived, it was fitting that everything be saved by a man not conceived. And therefore our

Lord sent the Holy Virgin the salvation by which he caused her to be with child and of which the angel said, 'Hail Mary, full of grace, the Lord is with thee'" (216–17). This satisfaction of the original sin is perfectly conveyed in the south portal, where the viewer can study the six scenes depicting the Creation of Adam and Eve (base of the trumeau, plate 12) and then join the three wise men (plate 9) presenting their gifts across the space of the portal to the infant Christ (plate 10).

The trumeau figure of the Virgin Mary became a devotional icon for local people, who would assemble before the portal at sunset, as a lantern hanging on a rope from the projecting voussoirs was lit. The hole drilled though the voussoirs to allow the passage of the rope can still be seen. In the gathering dusk the Virgin would gradually seem to detach herself from the surrounding narratives, standing as an isolated icon (plate 11).[26]

Here we find the most satisfying concordance between our two performances, sermon and portal. The preacher provides the words to accompany the devotion paid to the Mother of God, localized as Saint Mary of Amiens, telling his congregation what the sculptural program also reveals: the Virgin Mary *is* the church with its sacraments:

> Good gentlefolk, all of you together and each of you individually who recognize the Mother of God, Saint Mary of Amiens, which is your mother church, from which good comes, for to you come oil, chrism, baptism, extreme unction, burial, betrothal, marriage, [and] the blessed sacraments made in the holy church. (134)

> The Mother of God, Saint Mary of Amiens, is your lady of all ladies; she is the lady of the world, she is the queen of the glorious heavens, she is the treasure of sinners, she is the savior of souls,

she is the spouse of our Lord, she is the mother of Jesus Christ, she is the temple of the Holy Spirit. This Lady calls back to her those who have strayed, she sets the fallen on their feet, she is rescue to the captives. She comforts the sad, she strengthens the weak, she prays for the people, she sustains the despised, she guards women. Remember that sin entered the world through woman and that good is brought back to the world through woman. The reproach that Eve brought to woman was removed by the Virgin Mary, "since he whom the heavens could not contain, you have contained in your womb." This Lady is so lofty and of such power that she conceived in her womb what neither heavens nor earth could conceive: our Lord Jesus Christ; and for that good fortune let us gather on this day in the holy church, to the profit of our bodies and the salvation of our souls! (73–78)

# Conclusion

*Looking for "Reality"*

The parallels between the rhetoric of the preacher and the persuasiveness of the portals show that much is to be learned from the interface between the two performances—oral and visual; sermon and sculpture. Each is part of a coherent and multisensory projection of Catholic dogma to the people of Amiens, as both diocese and city.[1]

More difficult, however, is understanding how the words of the preacher might relate to what was going on "out there."[2] To consider the sermon a mirror of medieval society is obviously problematic. A successful preacher might have learned his métier from listening to others, from transcribing sermons as they were delivered, or from studying written transcripts. The result might draw more on long-established rhetorical traditions than on specific local problems or circumstances. Yet our preacher was surely experienced in interpreting and exploiting audience response. He might have experimented with various formulas and strategies until he found something that provoked the desired reaction—in short, something that worked. In this way the character of the audience might affect the preacher's performance. And that character might be found imprinted on the text.

What do we know about the people of Picardy in the later thirteenth century? Let us first briefly draw upon extraneous (secondary) sources to establish what is "known" about the local population, then return to our text in an attempt to extend and deepen our knowledge of this little-known segment of the medieval population, the country folk or *rustici*.

Picardy was one of the most fertile and densely populated areas of northern Europe. Its population had begun to grow rapidly as early as the late tenth century, thanks to the easily worked alluvial soil.[3] The availability of silver coinage allowed the population to purchase iron used to make saws, scythes, axes, and chisels, and improved iron-trimmed plows and mills.[4] By the twelfth century the large number of mills attested to the technological progress that linked improved agrarian productivity with a growing (although still relatively small) urban population partly engaged in commerce and industry, especially textile production. In this buoyant, technologically innovative society the architectural phenomenon that we call *Gothic* flourished.

Towns were not large; thirteenth-century Amiens had perhaps twenty thousand citizens in a province that numbered around a million.[5] Women probably constituted a slight majority. Most thirteenth-century people in Picardy lived in villages and hamlets—an essentially rural society that is hard for us to envisage, given the depopulated countryside of today. To believe that such rural folk were all animal-like peasants tied dumbly to endless rounds of work in the fields would be a serious mistake.[6] These were people engaged in a cash economy, and they probably had a keen sense of the value of their products and the profits to be made.[7] As the agrarian standard of living rose, aided by improvements in plows and mills and lively increases in the prices of commodities, especially grain, a rural landholder might be able to accumulate a small fortune. While some 10 to 15 percent of the population still lived a marginal existence, about 20 percent prospered.[8] The sermon's fund-raising agenda was clearly directed to the latter. That some of the members of the congregation might have commanded substantial resources is suggested by the preacher's allusion to scolding one's servant (182). The contributions of such people could make a real difference in the business of building the cathedral.

Amiens was the center of an agrarian hinterland, which it both served and exploited. The city had been granted a charter of liberties as a commune around 1100, placing it under the protection of the king. Urban prosperity was bound up with the commercial navigation of the Somme River, which allowed the export of locally produced woolen cloth and woad, employed as a blue dye. The urban population was sharply stratified: the leading bourgeois families, rich from textile production, trade, or commerce, were clearly separated from the *petits gens,* the ordinary folk, whose blue fingernails marked them as textile workers. Together with the rural population, these less privileged urban groups would have made up the majority of the faithful, to whom the cathedral project was in many ways geared.

In the mid thirteenth century the rates of increase in population growth and in the price of grain dropped.[9] At the same time the king was raising substantial taxes to finance the Crusade: such taxation, added to the economic weight of cathedral construction, may have contributed to the unrest that led to anticlerical manifestations documented in and around Amiens. In 1258, close to the date of our sermon text, scaffolding in the unfinished cathedral choir was destroyed by arson. Subsequent criminal proceedings implicated members of the bourgeoisie. Had a half century of continuous construction on the cathedral, coupled with adverse economic circumstances and increased taxes, led to damaged relations with members of the urban community? If so, the preacher may have been reaching out to an important constituency beyond the city: the wealthy rural population.

This leads to the second part of our discussion of "reality": the ways in which we can extract social meaning from the words of the preacher understood in relation to the cathedral sculpture. Students of medieval preaching have long recognized the existence of rhetorical modes, or carefully modulated styles of thought and oral delivery considered appropriate for this or that audience—in this case, the *rustici*.[10] Through the language and gestures employed, as well as the attitudes expressed, members of the audience might be able to find their own image and their own agenda in the performance of the preacher. When the preacher tells his congregation to go out into the fields and bring the sinners into church, he is assuming the role of Christ in relation to his apostles. His followers might be led to imitate him, just as the apostles imitated Christ.

Might the same principle apply to the problem of shaping and looking at sculpture? The designer of the sculptural program at Amiens has taken care to place motivational images well within the physical range (optical and tactile) of the visitor. The country person could relate the quatrefoil reliefs of the labors of the months in the dado of the portal of the saints to his own life, with its annual cycle determined by the agrarian activities of the var-

ious seasons. Likewise, the virtues and vices in the quatrefoils of
the central portal are directly available to the visitor—especially
the vices, placed at eye level, which the viewer could touch. And
we have seen that the saints, prophets, and apostles offer themselves to the gaze and to the intelligence not just as figures from
the distant past but as prototypes, models intended to induce the
visitor to embrace behavioral change.

This approach extends to questions of stylistic choice.[11] During the three decades of work on the sculpture, from 1220 to circa
1250, the "look" of the figures in the voussoirs and tympana, as
well as the column figures, was gradually transformed. Early experiments with elegant contrapposto "Antique style" figures, with
curved bodies and tightly crinkled folds, gave way to serial production of a more simple, vertical type. Moreover, scattered
throughout all three western portals, as well as in the column
figures of the south transept portal of the *Vierge dorée,* are stolid
round-faced, thick-necked types that art historians have traditionally dismissed as monotonous and ugly. Were these round-
faced sculptures intended to resemble ordinary thirteenth-century
people? Twelfth- and thirteenth-century works on image and
likeness endow the likeness with the dynamic force to impel it
toward its image or prototype. Thus, the visitor to the portal of
Saint Firmin, for example, might find himself in the image of the
saint and would be impelled forward toward his prototype.[12]

The preacher's intention was similar to that of the portal designers. Both seek to persuade ordinary folk to set themselves in
forward motion—to come to church and invoke its power, per-
sonified by the bishop and the Virgin Mary, to rescind the logic
of the earthly contract that links disobedience to final damnation
through inevitable cause and effect. The preacher complicates the

authority of contracts and oaths and calls into question the way in which wealth is accumulated and held. Instead of offering the glittering promise of a life entirely free from the corruption of all ties to material things (the Cathar heresy), he implies a mutation of the material world of dependency. One can reduce the pains of purgatory and the risk of eternal damnation—for both oneself and one's ancestors—not only by avoiding sin but also by offering alms to Our Lady, Saint Mary of Amiens. The preacher likens dependence on Saint Mary of Amiens to the peasant's dependence on the bounty of the fields, emphasizing local and material concerns. Offerings to Saint Mary also cancel the consequences of bad promises.

The idea of making a contract with Mary—obtaining pardon in return for a contribution—bespeaks an attitude to reciprocity that is heavily materialistic and quantitative. We may question whether this emphasis reflects the preacher's training or whether he was consciously mimicking the mentality of his audience. He was certainly most interested in counting. Thus, in the diocese of Amiens he counts 777 priests, 26 abbesses, 26 abbots, and 30 priories (3 and 163–67); for merely coming to church you get 40 days of pardon (31); for each mortal sin you owe 7 years of penance (93); to all benefactors of the church Mary gives 140 days of pardon (136, 155); pardon is worth more than this church filled with fine gold (92 and 154).

It is tempting to relate this passion for quantifying with a society increasingly locked in a dynamically changing protocapitalistic economy, one in which commodity values could not be fixed by any static idea of "just price" but were recognized as being determined by the market.[13] The preacher appeals to the congregation members' habit of assessing value in various exchanges. What a bargain to get pardon so easily when Saint Peter had to endure crucifixion for the same privilege!

Jacques Le Goff has discussed the process of adaptation by which the church came to terms with the idea of usury.[14] He saw the formalization of the concept of purgatory as propitious to nascent capitalism, since usurers, instead of going directly to hell, could now expect to go to purgatory, where salvific prayers of others might help: "The hope that hell might be avoided thanks to purgatory allowed the usurer to advance the economy and the society of the twelfth century toward capitalism."[15] Our preacher touches on the problem of usury when he insists that the principal sum of a loan must always be paid back in full, implying that the interest might be forgiven (223).

Our preacher was clearly caught in a dilemma. On the one hand, the story of Theophilus demonstrated Mary's power to thwart the devil, understood as the church's power to annul wrongful secular contracts. On the other hand, the preacher himself was raising money for a material church whose construction depended on a multitude of contracts, as well as for an institutional church whose wealth and power were based on a network of essentially contractual relationships. While projecting the contempt for material possessions associated with the apostolic church and the mendicants, he, like his audience, was fully engaged in the market economy.

We may watch our preacher wriggle! Having offered the bishop's absolution from "all the oaths *[seremens]* you have ever sworn," he immediately qualifies with two exceptions: oaths to take another's property or to reduce the power of the church (169–70). Then come two more promises of pardon from oaths (174 and 220), but the *seremens* involved are blasphemous exclamations, "by God's wounds!" and the like. There are three more promises of pardon, one offering freedom from "foolish undertakings [*foles fiances*]," as long as they did not involve seizing another's property or disinheriting someone (221). And finally we have the promise of pardon from unreasonable legal suits (*coses terrienes*) for those who offer their gifts to Saint Mary of Amiens (226).

Do we detect a sleight of hand on the part of the preacher, who seems to be taking advantage of his audience's tendency to think in terms of reaping profit from an exchange? The services he offers for hard cash might seem to us somewhat illusory, and the principal offense (blasphemy) negligible, but the exchange must be understood within the framework of a highly charged subject—namely, the notion of purgatory, or the continuing existence of people after they die and before they go to heaven.

Insisting on the potential impact of one's behavior and penance on the fate of ancestors suspended in the fires of purgatory, the preacher participates in one of the most powerful theological movements of his period. Le Goff has traced the formalization of the idea of purgatory—indeed, the very use of the noun *purgatory*—to the theologians and preachers associated with Notre-Dame of Paris in the late twelfth century.[16] The concept was most popular with the ordinary folk, and it was projected mainly through sermons. Our sermon contains nine references to purgatory (136, 137, 138, 139 [twice], 140, 141, 142, 150). The word *pardon* occurs more than fifty times—on average, once a minute. The word *purgatory* is concentrated in a single part of the sermon, as the preacher projects the power of the church with its sacraments and its bishop who can lead the faithful to heaven and who offers the pardons necessary to reduce the sufferings of purgatory for members of the audience and their forebears. The first use of the word comes in the very sentence that offers 140 days of pardon from the fires of purgatory to the benefactors of the church of Notre-Dame Saint Mary of Amiens. Then follows a series of agonizing illustrations of the pains inflicted by the fires of purgatory, which are more rigorous than the worst tortures that can be imagined on earth. The preacher even explains the derivation of the word (from *purgare,* "to purge"; 139).

The church made several important gains with the new dogma. It provided a formidable weapon against heretics, since Cathars denied the existence of purgatory. It allowed the church exclusive control over the business of dying and over mediation between the living and the dead. Soon after the period of our sermon, the clergy of Amiens Cathedral began to add lateral chapels to the nave in order to provide liturgical space for private masses for the wealthy dead. And finally, of course, confession, penance, and masses for the dead (the *trentel* mentioned by the preacher, 167) became ways in which devout living persons could mitigate the effects of the fires of purgatory on their beloved forebears.[17]

The Last Judgment portal, like the *Mère Dieu* portal, provides the most recognizably Gothic elements of the cathedral; such portals are the figurative counterparts of the flying buttress or the rib vault. The great central Last Judgment portal of the west facade of Notre-Dame of Paris, in many ways a prototype for the one at Amiens, was designed in the same febrile intellectual environment that saw what Le Goff called the birth of purgatory.[18] Gothic architecture and sculpture may be understood largely in terms of a newly energized projection of Catholic dogma to the rural population; this was a mission where preaching played a particularly important role. The power of the church as mediator between the living and the dead in purgatory; the conflation of the identity and role of the Virgin Mary with the church; the elusive promise of the new contract; the spectacular new forms of Gothic architecture, with its painted sculpture and glass— these were some of the weapons used to wage the battle for the hearts and the minds of the people.

. . .

It is time now to join the little congregation and listen to the preacher. In the sermon that follows, readers will find support for their various views on the role of the church in medieval society. Some may chuckle at the gullibility of simple-minded folk seduced by the preacher's repertoire of cheap tricks to exchange hard-earned currency for illusory rewards for themselves and their ancestors in purgatory. Such readers will be reminded of the cynicism expressed by Chaucer's pardoner as he plied his trade and will anticipate the discrediting of the sale of indulgences, some two and half centuries after our text, with Martin Luther and the Reformation.

Other readers, however, might recognize that the exploitation of the many by the few is a characteristic of all societies—not least our own. The question, it seems to me, is not whether people are exploited (they always are) but rather under what circumstances exchanges took place and what the exchange actually purchased. Our preacher offers positive as well as negative incentives (carrots and sticks), and he is unfailingly courteous to the members of his audience, carefully reinforcing their self-image. He provides an accurate account of the rewards to be obtained in return, just as the sculptural program of the cathedral portals offers a kind of product guide to what is available inside. First, one will find the opportunity to construct a life according to a coherent code that offers the hope of change, whereby things do not need to end as badly as they began. Second, one will gain the services of an institution that provides critical rites of passage at birth, marriage, and death, not to mention the sense of community inherent in the Eucharistic sacrament and the engaging local traditions, stories, and images associated with the saints.[19] And third, there is the Virgin Mary—not just any Virgin, but Saint Mary of Amiens: one's very own, most powerful, champion.

And of course, we should not forget the light and color, the forms and spaces of the Gothic cathedral, whose central spire, carrying the relics of the local saints, formed a visual point of reference for the eyes of country folk working in the fields of the Picard plain and whose bells provided a temporal framework for their working day.

With these thoughts I invite you, the reader, to lend your eyes for seeing and your ears for hearing and your heart for remembering, as we allow the preacher now to speak for himself.

Plate 1    The three portals (west facade), general view

Plate 2 Central (Last Judgment) portal, general view

Plate 3   Central portal, left side

Column figures *(left to right):* Habakkuk and Nahum (minor prophets, on the buttress); Daniel and Ezekiel (major prophets); six apostles, with Paul last. In the door jamb, the wise virgins; in the central trumeau, Christ the *Beau Dieu,* with David or Solomon below. In the voussoirs, the elect; in the lintel, the resurrection of the dead. On the quatrefoils: prophecies (beneath the prophets); virtues and vices (beneath the apostles).

Plate 4    Central portal, right side

Column figures: Six apostles, with Peter on the right. In the door jamb, the wise virgins; in the central trumeau, Christ the *Beau Dieu,* with David or Solomon below. In the voussoirs, the elect; in the lintel, the resurrection of the dead. On the quatrefoils, virtues and vices.

Plate 5　Central portal, tympanum

Lower lintel: Angels blowing trumpet of Last Judgment; resurrection of the
dead; weighing of the saved and the damned. Upper lintel: The damned *(right)*
entering the jaws of hell; the saved *(left)*, led by Saints Francis and Peter, entering the celestial city. Tympanum: Christ, son of man, as Judge, flanked by
Mary and John; in the tip, the apocalyptic Christ.

Plate 6    North (Saint Firmin) portal, left embrasure

Column figures *(left to right):* Zechariah and Haggai (minor prophets, on the buttress); Ulphe; angel; Ache; Acheul; angel; Bishop Honoratus(?). On the quatrefoils: prophecies (beneath the prophets); signs of the zodiac and labors of the months (beneath the saints).

Plate 7    North portal, right embrasure

Column figures *(left to right):* Bishop Firmin the Confessor(?); Domice; Bishop Sauve(?); Fuscien; Gentien; Victoric(?); Zephaniah (minor prophet, on the buttress). On the quatrefoils: signs of the zodiac; labors of the months; prophecies of Zephaniah.

Plate 8   North portal, tympanum

Lower lintel: Six seated bishops; in the middle, reliquary (of Saint Firmin?).
Upper lintel: Bishop Sauve discovering the lost relics of Saint Firmin *(center)*;
townsfolk from neighboring cities. Tympanum: Procession with the relics back
to Amiens; Green Man *(left)*. In the central trumeau, Saint Firmin.

Plate 9     South *(Mère Dieu)* portal, left embrasure

Column figures *(left to right):* Obadiah (minor prophet, on the buttress); Sheba; Solomon; Herod; the three magi. On the quatrefoils: scenes relating to Solomon and Sheba; arrival of the magi; prophecies of Obadiah.

Plate 10    South portal, right embrasure

Column figures *(left to right):* Archangel Gabriel and Mary (Annunciation);
Elizabeth and Mary (Visitation); Infant Christ and Simeon (Presentation);
Amos and Joel (minor prophets, on the buttress). On the quatrefoils: scenes from
the infancy of Christ with John the Baptist; prophecies of Amos and Joel.

Plate 11  South portal, trumeau, the Virgin Mary
*(Mère Dieu)* and Child

Plate 12    South portal, base of trumeau, the story of
Adam and Eve

Eve created from Adam's rib *(top);* eating the apple *(middle);* Adam digs while
Eve spins *(bottom).*

Plate 13    South portal, tympanum

Lower lintel: Six seated Old Testament patriarchs and prophets; in the middle,
the Ark of the Covenant. Upper lintel: Dormition *(left)* and Assumption *(right)*
of the Virgin Mary. Tympanum: Triumph of the Virgin.

Plate 14    South transept portal, general view

Column figures: saints. In the trumeau, a replica of the *Vierge dorée;* in the lowest lintel, the mission of the apostles; in the upper lintels and tympanum, miracles of Saint Honoratus.

Plate 15    South transept, *Vierge dorée*

Carved c. 1250 for the trumeau of the portal (see replica in plate 14); now attached to a pier inside the south transept.

# Sermon in Honor
of the Mother of God,
Saint Mary of Amiens

*Text and Translation*

1      Bele douce gent, tant poi de vous comme il a repairié
à sainte eglise en l'onner la glorieuse mere diu sainte
Marie d'Amiens, qui est nostre mere eglise, dont vous
tenés oile et cresme et bauptesme, noces et mariages,
enoliement, enterrement, sains sacremens en est fais
en sainte eglise.

2      Il m'i convenra parler car à ciaus et à celes qui n'i sont
ge n'i parlerai mie.

3      Bele douce gent, me sire l'evesques d'Amiens, qui est
nostre sire esperitueus et qui est ou lieu nostre segneur
en terre, manda et commanda à vo segneur de prestre
et à tous les autres prestres qui sont en son evesquié,
dont il i a VIIc et XLXXVII [*recte* LXXVII], que en
quelconques lieu les beneoites reliques et li mesage
de l'eglise d'Amiens venroient, que li iour et les festes
fusent gardées entierement, si hautement comme le
saint ior de noel et comme le saint ior de pasques et
de saint diemence en vertu de sainte obedience, des-
troitement, seur paine d'escommeniement.

4      Que dex vous beneie!

5      Vos sire de prestres a il fait le commandement mon
segneur l'evesque? Certes, maistre, oïl par mon chief.
Il a fait que sages, que saciés entierement que si tost
comme il fust aperceus qu'il eust pechié en trespasse-
ment du commandement de sainte obedience, il deust
avoir depoillié et osté de seur lui les benoites armes
nostre segneur, comme la casure et l'amit, et l'aube,
et l'estole dusca l'eure qu'il eust esté à sainte confession
et à sainte repentance des commandemens qu'il aroit
trespassés de sainte obedience.

1 Good gentlefolk, as few of you as have gathered in the holy church in honor of the glorious Mother of God, Saint Mary of Amiens, which is our mother church, from which you have received the oil of chrism and baptism, marriage, extreme unction, burial, and the holy sacraments that are made in the holy church.

2 It is to you that I should speak, since to the men and women who are not here I cannot speak at all.

3 Good gentlefolk, my lord the bishop of Amiens, who is our spiritual lord in place of our Lord on earth, has ordered and commanded your lord priest and all the other priests who are in his diocese, of whom there are 777, that in whatever place the blessed relics and the word of the church of Amiens should come, the days and the celebrations should be observed fully, as highly as the holy day of Christmas, the holy day of Easter, and the holy Sunday, and strictly, by virtue of holy obedience, on pain of excommunication.

4 May God bless you!

5 Your lord the priest, has he obeyed my lord the bishop? Certainly, master; yes, upon my head! He has acted wisely, and you should all know that as soon as he were to perceive that he had sinned against the commandment of holy obedience, he would have to strip and remove from him the blessed insignia of our Lord, including the chasuble, the miter, the alb, and the stole, until he had been to holy confession and holy repentance of the commandments of holy obedience he had broken.

6    Que sachiés entierement que si li prestres estoit inobe-
     diens, il seroit inregulers, et se il estoit inregulers, il ne
     troveroit archevesque ne evesque ne prestre curé qui
     l'en carchast penitance, ne qui digneté en eust, dusque
     il aroit parlé à l'apostoile de Rome dont dex nous dist
     cele parole par la bouche de Samuel le profete: *Maior
     est obedientia quam victima;* li autre dient *quem victime,*
     et nequedent bon est et l'un et l'autre.

7    Saciés entierement que tant est forschose de trespasser
     obedience, qu'il n'est aucuns d'ome ne de fame qui le
     seust penser, ne langue qui le seust descrire.

8    Dont nous trovons en l'escriture que li homs et la fame
     qui hui en cest ior est demorés en son terrien labourage,
     il est demorés malvaisement et seur escons et seur le
     trespassement de sainte obedience; dont nous trovons
     que li hom et la fame qui hui en cest ior est demourés
     il peche tout autrestant comme fist Eve et Adans qui
     mengierent la pome que nostre segneur leur avoit
     deffendu qu'il n'en goutassent.

9    Bele douce gent, saciés par bone verité que pour tant
     seulement que Adans et Eve trespasserent le comman-
     dement d'obedience, il furent Vc ans et XIIII en la
     mort et en le passion d'enfer, dont dex nous gart tous
     et toutes par sa grant pité et par sa grant misericorde!

10   Biaus amis et tu bele amie, nostre segneur nous dist
     ceste parole: *Ubi te invenero, ibi te iudicabo.*

11   Si m'aiut dex!

6    You should be quite sure that if the priest were disobe-
     dient, he would [be considered] irregular, and being
     so, would find no archbishop or bishop or priest who
     would not charge him to repent, no matter what his
     rank, even if he had spoken with the pope in Rome.
     Of whom God has given us this word by the mouth
     of Samuel the prophet, "Obedience is better than sacri-
     fice"; others say, "than sacrifices," and nevertheless one
     is as good as the other.

7    Know entirely that such is the folly of disobedience
     that there is no man or woman who could think of it,
     nor tongue that could describe it.

8    Of which we find in Scripture that the man and the
     woman who on this day kept working in their field
     have remained there wrongly, in hiding and in breach
     of holy obedience. From which we find that the man
     and the woman who stayed away on this day sin just
     as Eve and Adam when they ate the apple that our
     Lord had forbidden them to taste.

9    Good gentlefolk, you should know in good truth that
     just because Adam and Eve broke the commandment
     of obedience, they were 514 years in death and in the
     agonies of hell—from which may God save us all, men
     and women, by his great pity and by his great mercy!

10   Good friend, and you, my good lady friend, our Lord
     said unto us, *Ubi te invenero, ibi te iudicabo.*

11   So help me God!

12    Nostre segneur dist par cele parole: Pechierres, fait
      nostre segneur *là u ge te troverai, là te iugerai.* Or sacés
      entierement que cil et celes qui sont demoré en cel point
      comme ge vous ai devisé, il seront malvaisement pris
      que saciés par bone verité que s'il estoient pris en la
      piece de terre sans confession et sans repentance, il
      seroient iugié à la mort et la passion d'enfer, tant
      com dex sera dex, ne ià merci dex n'en ara.

13    Or me faites pais! Que de la beneoite bouche dont dex
      dist *consummatum est* soit la bouche benoite que iamais
      ne puist ele estre abeurée de si dolereus morsel comme
      de mort dusca icele eure que il ait recheu vraie con-
      fession. Qui pais me prestera et qui de bon cuer
      m'escoutera.

14    *Probatio dilectonis exibitio est operit [recte operis], dixit
      beatus Gregorius.*

15    [f. 131v] Me sires sains Gregoires nous dist par ceste
      parole que par la vraie amour que li uns a vers l'autre
      connoist on son ami, et par l'uevre connoist on le bon
      ouvrier.

16    Sachiés par bone verité, li apostres nous raconte, qui-
      conques aime diu, il ot volentiers de lui parler; mais
      li malvais crestiens ou la malvaise crestiene qui deu
      n'aime ne croit, il sont pieur que tirant qui deu batirent
      à l'estache ne qui le crucefierent; que l'escriture nos
      raconte que endementiers que nostre segneur diu par-
      loit as tirans qui le crucefioient, que il estoupoient lor
      nés et lor orelles, car il lor sanloit que la parole nostre
      segneur puïst et sa beneoite precieuse char.

12    Thus said our Lord: "Sinner," said our Lord, "there,
      where I find you, there I shall judge you." Know, there-
      fore, and doubt not, that the men and women who
      stayed away, as I said, will be taken in an evil hour.
      Know in good sooth that if they were taken on their
      land without having confessed their sins and repented,
      they would be condemned to death and suffer the pangs
      of hell; as God is God, he shall not spare them.

13    Now hearken well! May the blessed mouth of God
      which said, "It is finished," bless the one who shall not
      suffer the pangs of death before receiving true confes-
      sion: whoever marks my words and who listens to me
      with a good heart.

14    "The proof of a person's love is [found in] his works,"
      said Saint Gregory.

15    My lord Saint Gregory told us thereby that a man knows
      his friends by the true love they bear him, and that a
      good worker is known by his works.

16    Know in good truth, says the apostle, that whoever loves
      God gladly hears him spoken of, but bad Christians,
      men or women, who neither love God nor believe in
      him are worse than the tyrants who beat God at the
      whipping post or those who crucified him. The scrip-
      tures tell us that when our Lord God spoke to the
      tyrants who crucified him they blocked up their noses
      and ears, because it seemed to them that the word of
      our Lord and his blessed precious flesh stank.

17 Tout ausi est il de chiaus et de cheles qui sont demouré.

Il lor sanle que la parole dieu lor pue; et saciés sans nule
doute il en arent encore avec tout ce une si dolereuse
maleicon, que d'orient dusque en occident il n'i ara
arcevesque, ne evesque, ne ermite, ne reclus, ne prieus,
ne abé, ne prestre curé, ne capelain, ne iacobin, ne cor-
deler, ne moine blanc ne noir, ne gris, diacre ne sous
diacre, ne none blanche ne noire, ne cardonal de Rome,
sus l'apostole meisme, pour tant que il dient l'eure de
prime, qu'il ne soient maudit de toutes les langues
qui furent le saint sacrement de nostre segneur.

18 Que saciés que nus prestres ne seroit si hardis qu'il osast
messe canter dusc'à cele eure qu'il soit maudit en tous
les sacremens qui sont fait de nostre segneur de chief
en chief, fors seulement à II, qui sont les II la nuit du
Noel, que on chante une messe à mie nuit et l'autre au
point du ior.

19 Saciés à ces II messes il n'i sont pas maudit; car à ces II
messes n'a point de prime; mais à toutes les autres, par
toutes les eglises, là où prime est, est chantée et messé.

20 Veés et oiés la parole que Dex en dist par la bouche
David le profete: *Increpasti superbos maledicti qui declinant a mandatis tuis.*

21 Biaus sire dex, fait David par la bouche nostre segneur
del saint pooir que tu as en ciel et en terre, et del saint
pooir à ta douce mere et de tous sains et de toutes, de
toute la bele compaignie de paradis, soient tout cil et
toutes celes maudit, qui defalent à tes commandemens.

17    It is the same with those men and women who have
      stayed away. It seems to them that the word of God
      stinks; and you should know without any doubt that
      they shall be so grievously cursed that from the east
      to the west there will be no archbishop, bishop, hermit,
      recluse, prior, abbot, priest, curate, chaplain, Dominican
      or Franciscan, white or black or gray monk, deacon or
      subdeacon, white or black nun, or cardinal of Rome
      under the pope himself, for all they observe the hour
      of prime, who would not be cursed in all the tongues
      in which our Lord's holy sacrament is said.

18    Know, then, that no priest shall be so bold as to sing the
      mass as long as he is cursed in all the sacraments which
      are made entirely of our Lord himself, except only those
      two [masses] of the night of Christmas, of which one is
      sung at midnight and the other at dawn.

19    Know that at these two masses they are not accursed,
      since in neither is there any prime, but in all other masses
      [they are], in all churches where prime is chanted and
      mass celebrated.

20    See and hear the word of God through the mouth
      of David his prophet, "Thou hast rebuked the proud;
      they are cursed who decline from thy commandments."

21    "Good Lord God!" said David, "By the mouth of our
      Lord, with the holy power you have in heaven and on
      earth and the holy power of your sweet mother and all
      the saints, male and female, and all the beautiful com-
      pany of paradise, may all those men and women who
      disobey your commandments be cursed."

22 Beles gent, nostre segneur nous demonstre par ceste
parole: *Dilige proximum tuum sicut te ipsum;* saciés par
bone verité nostre segneur nous dist et commande par
ceste raison: "Aime ton proisme et comme toi meisme,"
ce dist nostre sires, vous amis et tu bele amie, se tu vois,
ne ses, ne aperchois le damage de ton voisin ne de ton
proisme prochain, fai li savoir que tout isi le commande
nostre segneur et ge le vous di de sa part; et se vous m'en
volés desmentir, si l'en desmentés.

23 Que si me puist il aidier isi le croi ge; ausi font toute
maniere de bone gent.

24 Et se il i a chaiens aucun home ou aucune fame qui tout
isi ne le croit, mal i soit il venus; à bone estrine que ge
di qu'il n'est pas bons crestiens; enten bien ceste parole.

25 Ore, bele douce gent, vous connoissiés vus voisins et
savés mex là u il mainent que ge ne sai, et là u il sont
que ge ne sai.

26 Ge vous dirai que vous me ferés: vous presterés vos cors
et vos menbres à la mere dieu sainte Marie, et si le ferés
une petite bonté qui ne vous coustera denier ne obole,
ne qui le poist, ne qui le vaille; et si ferés I pelerinage
en l'onor de cel precieus pelerinage que nostre segneur
dieu fist du pretoire Pilate dusques en sont le mont de
Cauvaire; que saciés que onques li dous dieus n'i passa
I tout seul pas que il n'i fust férus ou boutés ou escopis,
où, sachiés? En mi son beneoit visage.

22 Good people, thus says our Lord, *Dilige proximum tuum sicut te ipsum:* know in good truth that our Lord said and commanded with the word, "Love your neighbor as thyself." Thus said our Lord. Therefore you, my friend, and you, my good lady friend, if you see or perceive the harm done by your neighbor or one close to you, let him know that the Lord so commands, and I am telling you this on his behalf; and if you wish to contradict me, you deny him.

23 For if he can help me, then I believe him; that's what all sorts of good people say.

24 And if there be any man or woman here who does not believe this, may evil come to him; I say with good reason that he is not a good Christian; listen well to this word.

25 Now, good gentlefolk, you know your neighbors and know better than I do where they live and where they are.

26 I will tell you what you will do for me: you must lend your body and your legs to Saint Mary, the Mother of God, and you must render her a little service which will not cost you a penny or halfpenny, or anything of that weight or worth: that is, go on a pilgrimage in honor of the precious pilgrimage that our Lord made from Pilate's court to Mount Calvary; know that with every step the sweet Lord took he was beaten or kicked and spat at—do you know where? In the middle of his blessed face!

27 Et si vous commant en remission de vos pechiés et en
penitance, [f. 132] que vous ne dites mie: "Venés au
moustier! venés au moustier!" sans raison, qu'il ne
vous feroient se gaber non; mais alés tout belement là
où vous les sarés, et si lor blasmés lor folies, et si lor
dites le damage qu'il pueent rechevoir, et le gaaig qu'il
i puent conquerre.

28 Car sachiés tout avant, me sire li evesques lor fait pardon et absolution de toutes les festes que il ont mal
gardées.

29 Ce n'est pas corvée qu'il feront à la douce mere diu
sainte Marie; or prenés garde entre vous, se vous avés
bien gardées les festes, que vous a commandées tout
l'an contreval.

30 Si m'aït dex! Ge cuit qu'il i a moult à amender.

31 Après i gaaigniés vous encore qui mex vaut, que pour
seulement venir de leurs maisons au mostier, il gaai-
gnent XL iornées de vrai pardon, sans doner denier
ne obole, et XL iornées de vrai pardon, pour atendre
le besoigne le douce mere diu sainte Marie que ele soit
aconsomée.

32 Car saciés certainement c'on puet bien venir à la court
sans congié, mais on ne s'en puet ne ne doit venir sans
congié.

33 Or i alés, quiconques veult dusc'à XIIII [*recte* IIII], ou
dusc'à VI, et vous gaaignerés X iornées de vrai pardon;
de tant serés plus aprochié de la gloire de paradis que
vous n'estiés.

27 And so I command you, that your sins may be forgiven, that you never say, "Come to church! Come to church!" without giving a reason, lest you be mocked. But go roundly there where you know they are, and denounce their foolishness and tell them the harm they might incur and the gain they might receive.

28 For you should know above all that my lord the bishop will grant them pardon and absolution for all the feasts that they have failed to observe.

29 What they do for the sweet Mother of God, Saint Mary, will not go unrewarded. Now, take a good look at yourselves, at whether you have observed the feast days prescribed for the past year.

30 May God help me! I think that there is much to amend.

31 Afterward you will have won something worth even more, for by simply coming to church from home, they accrue forty days of true pardon, without giving a penny or halfpenny, and forty days of true pardon for meeting the needs of the [church of the] sweet Mother of God, Saint Mary, that she [or it] be fulfilled [or completed].

32 Now make no mistake: you are free to come to court but you cannot and should not come without permission.

33 For by coming you will earn up to four or six [days], and you will receive ten days of true pardon; you will be that much closer to the glory of paradise than you were before.

34 Sachiés quant vous i venistes et à cascun pas que vous i
passerés alant et venant, ce soit en estaignement contre
cascun faus pas de pechié que vous avés passé et fait
contre la volenté Ihesu Crist et sa douce chiere mere;
et à cascune parole que vous i parlerés, che soit encontre
une fause parole que vous avés dite de vo bouche contre
la volenté nostre segneur: que nostre segneur par la priere
de sa douce mere li vous vuelle pardoner!

35 Et tant d'omes et tant de fames comme vous i amenrés,
nostre segneur de tantes courones vous veille couronner
en sa gloire.

36 Dites "Amen" que dex le vous otroit par sa grant pitié et
par sa grant misericorde.

37 Veés, bele douce gent, traiés-vous cha plus pres de moi,
et si faites à la mere diu sainte Marie, pour toutes les
bontés que ele vous fesist onques une bonté qui ne vous
coustera denier ne obole, que vous vous traiés cha plus
près de moi, et si me prestés vos ex pour veoir et vos
oreilles por escouter et vos cuers por bien retenir; car
saciés en verité, parole mal entendue mal est rendu,
et par ceste raison le vous proverai.

38 Sachiés ge ai esté en maint lieu, et moult ai oï aucune
fois quant cil home et ces fames repairoient d'aucun
preudome qui avoit son cors deronpu et sa teste à aus
ensaignier la voie de verité, et saciés par une oreille
lor entroit et par l'autre lor isoit, et donc dient li uns à
l'autre: dex, dame sainte Marie, com cest preudon a bien
sarmoné! Et c'a il dit? fait li uns à l'autre. En non diu,
ge ne sai. Or poés bien savoir comme il i a prest le cuer
pour retenir et les ex pour resgarder et oreilles pour oïr.

34    Know that when you come here, for every step you take
      in coming and going, there will be an atonement for
      every false step you have taken in the past, sinning
      against the will of Jesus Christ and his sweet dear
      mother, and that every word you speak here will
      counter an untruth spoken by you against the will
      of our Lord: may our Lord, through the prayers of
      his sweet mother, grant you pardon!

35    And for every man and woman you bring to church,
      may our Lord crown you with as many crowns of glory.

36    Say "Amen!" [and] may God of his great pity and his
      great mercy grant it to you.

37    Come, good gentlefolk, draw closer to me, and for all
      the goodness she has rendered you, do for the Mother
      of God, Saint Mary, an act of goodness that will not cost
      a penny or a halfpenny; draw closer to me, and lend me
      your eyes for seeing and your ears for hearing and your
      hearts for remembering, for you should know in truth
      that a word poorly understood is poorly delivered,
      and I shall prove it to you with this reason.

38    Know that I have traveled far and wide, and I once
      heard much from some men and women who had just
      come back from some wild-haired, tattered fellow [a
      preacher] teaching the way of truth. What he said went
      in one ear and out the other of those who heard him.
      "God, Holy Mary!" said one to the other, "How well
      this man has preached!" "What did he say?" the one
      went to the other. "In God's name, I don't know." So
      you can see how he'd lent his heart for remembering
      and his eyes for seeing and his ears for hearing!

39   *Non incipienti sed perseveranti dabitur corona.*

40   Bele douce gent, l'escriture nous ensaigne que i a nus hom ne nule fame, pour bon commencement que il aient, n'aront haute corone en paradis, se il n'a bone fin.

41   Proiés nostre segneur que à bone fin nous atraie.

42   Et orendroit le vous mosterai par vive raison.

43   Sachiés par bone verité que Judas qui nostre segneur dieu traï, il eut moult bon commencement; car, sachiés, il fu uns des XII apostres nostre segneur, et preecha la foi, et longement ensievi nostre segneur. Sachiés en verité que au deerrain il fu de si foible foi et de si povre creanche, qu'il ne peut contester as tentasions du diable, qui moult est plains de grant engieng, car il est espiritueus et trebucha du chiel par son orguel. Ne iamais orguellieus en paradis ne montera.

44   Vous devés avoir humelité contre orguel, douçor [f. 132v] et amour contre felenie.

45   Ausi eut nostre segneur; saciés en verité, oir porrés grant misericorde de nostre segneur; nostre sire aime el felon le nature qu'il fist, car ele est bone; mais il het le felenie, dont il est, car ele est male.

46   Or oés por diu que nostre sire dist à Judas que il vousist bien qu'il se repentist de la felenie et de la traïson qu'il avoit porparlée.

47   Amis, fist nostre segneur à Judas, *ad quod venisti?*

48   Fai ce que tu a quis; i'aim toi, et tu hes moi.

39    "The crown is given not for the starting but for the
      persevering."

40    Good gentlefolk, the scriptures teach us that no man
      and no woman, no matter how well they begin, will
      have their lofty crown in paradise unless they have
      a good ending.

41    Pray to our Lord that he grants us a good end.

42    And now let me explain that with a lively reason.

43    Know in good truth that Judas, who betrayed our
      Lord, had a very good start, for he was one of the
      twelve apostles of our Lord and preached the faith
      and followed our Lord for a long time. Know in truth
      that in the end his faith was so feeble and his belief so
      poor that he could not resist the temptations of the devil,
      who is full of great cunning; for he was a spiritual being
      who fell from heaven because of his pride. The proud
      shall never ascend to heaven.

44    You should have humility as opposed to pride, sweetness
      and love as opposed to perfidy.

45    Our Lord had such [humility]. You should know in
      truth you can receive the great mercy of our Lord. He
      loves sinner's being, which he made, for it is good; but
      he hates his perfidy, for it is evil.

46    Now in the name of the Lord, hear that our Lord called
      upon Judas to repent of his sins and of the treason he
      had committed.

47    "My friend," said our Lord to Judas, "Whereto art thou
      come?

48    "Do as you must. I love you, and you hate me."

49 Sachiés certainement, onques Judas ne s'amolia envers nostre segneur, ains le livra es mains des tirans.

50 Et quant Judas vit les grans hontes et les persecutions c'on faisoit à nostre segneur, si se desespera: Ha! las! maleureus, fist-il adonques, c'ai ge fait, qui ai traï mon segneur! Ge ai fait si grant pechié qu'il pas pooir de moi pardonner!

51 Certes il mena comme malvais lerres; que nus n'est el monde si grans pechierres, s'il se veult à nostre segneur acorder par vraie confession et par sainte repentance, que deus tantost ses pechiés ne li pardoint.

52 Ausi eust eu Judas vrai pardon, s'il l'eust requis à nostre segneur, mais il n'osa; ains li entra li diables el cors, qu'il avoit servi, si s'ala pendre; dont l'ame de son cors fu dampnée perpetueument.

53 Or proiés nostre segneur que de malvaise covoitise, et de mauvaise envie, et de male haine, et de male desesperance nous gart et deffende par sa grant pitié et par sa grant misericorde.

*De Magdalena* [added in red in main text]

54 Or faites pais, bele douce gent, que nostre segneur vous prest et sa pais et s'amour.

49 Know truly that Judas did not take pity on our Lord, and so he delivered him into the hands of the tyrants.

50 And when Judas saw the great shame and the suffering brought against our Lord, he despaired. "Alas! wretch that I am," he said, "what have I done, I who have betrayed my Lord? I have committed so great a sin that he cannot pardon me!"

51 Indeed, he behaved like a wicked thief; but no one in the world is so great a sinner that if he wishes to reconcile with our Lord by true confession and holy repentance, the Lord will not forgive his sins at once.

52 And so Judas might have had true pardon if he had asked it of our Lord, but he did not dare; and so the devil whom he had served entered into his body; he went and hanged himself, for which the soul of his body was forever damned.

53 Now pray to our Lord that he guard and save us with his great pity and great mercy from wicked lust, from wicked envy, from wicked hatred, and from wicked despair.

### On Mary Magdalene

54 Now be at peace, good gentlefolk, for our Lord offers you his peace and his love.

55 Sachiés par bone verité, la douce Masalaine, ele ot moult malvais commencement, mais ele eut moult bone fin; car l'escriture nous raconte que ele estoit si pecheris que ele estoit entechiée des VII pechiéus mortieus et des VII diables tous vis avoit dedens son cors; mais sachiés entierement ele n'estoit pas desesperée de nostre segneur, ains avoit dedens soi une bone teche et une bone maniere, qui trestous les malvaises teches vaincoit. Car la damoisele manoit en charité. Et sachiés quiconques maint en charité, ce dist l'escriture, dex maint en lui.

56 Bele douce gent, sachiés que nous trouvons en l'escriture que quant la bele Masalaine aloit à son pechié, tos iors avoit ses mains aouvertes à faire aumosnes, et metoit es mains as povres si coiement et si sinplement que ia nus ne le veist ne ne seust, là où ele peust, fors nostre segneur dieu, et tout dis disoit au povre nostre segneur, quant ele li donoit s'aumosne: Tenés por l'amour dieu, proiés nostre segneur qu'il me giet de *[word obliterated]* pechié

57 Hé! Si m'aït dieu! Ele donoit s'aumosne selonc les dis de l'escriture; car l'escriture nous raconte: *Qui facit elemosinam, nesciat sinistra tua quid faciat dextera tua:* quant tu fais aumosne, fait l'escriture, garde que ta senestre mains ne sache que fait la destre.

58 Biaus amis et tu bele amie, n'enten pas com parole de tes mains, eles pas n'ont entendement: moult porroiés faire de malisse devant eles anchois que eles t'encusassent.

55    Know in good truth that the sweet Magdalene started
      very badly but ended very well; for we learn from the
      scriptures that she was so great a sinner that she was
      infected with the seven mortal sins and that the seven
      devils all lived in her body. But you should know for
      certain that she did not despair of our Lord, for she
      had within her good qualities and a good disposition,
      which conquered all the evil in her. For the young lady
      remained charitable. And as the scriptures tell us, God
      dwells within all who remain charitable.

56    Good gentlefolk, the scriptures tell us that even when
      the good Magdalene was a sinner, she constantly opened
      her hands to give alms, placing them in the hands of the
      poor people so gently and so simply, wherever she could,
      that nobody except our Lord God could see or know,
      and always as she gave alms she said to our Lord's poor
      people, "Take this, for the love of God; pray God to
      keep me from sin."

57    Ha! May God help me! She gave alms according to
      the words of the scripture, for the scripture tells us, *Qui
      facit elemosinam, nesciat sinistra tua quid faciat dextera
      tua:* "When thou dost alms," says the scripture, "let not
      thy left hand know what thy right hand doth."

58    Good friend, and you, my good lady friend, do not
      follow the temptation your hands incur; they do not
      have any understanding; you can do much evil in their
      presence before they will accuse you.

59    Saches tu vraiement par la destre entent-on nostre
      segneur et sa gloire, et par la senestre le monde et le
      beubant, dont il i a moult et asés.

60    La douche Masalaine donoit s'aumosne selonc diu, ele
      ne le donoit pas selonc le monde et sachiés ele en ot sa
      merite en paradis la sus amont.

61    *Dimissa sunt ei peccata quoniam dilexit multum.*

62    Et fist nostre segneur à Marie Madeleine, ge te pardoins
      tes pechiés.

63    Bele douce gent, sachiés par bone verité que par la bone
      repentanche qu'ele ot et par la bone fin, nostre segneur
      le corona en paradis avec ses apostres et avec sa bele
      compaignie, et l'escriture nous monstre que ele est
      *Aposto* [f. 133] *la apostolorum.*

64    Bele bele *[sic]* douce gent, or prions nostre segneur que
      à bone fin et à bone repentance et à vraie confession
      nous atraie par sa grant pitié et par sa grant misericorde.

65    Bele douce gent, entendés bien ceste parole: *Qui hon-*
      *orem honorem, et qui tributum tributum,* ce dist li sages.

66    Li sages dist c'on doit prendre garde qui on honeure et
      qui on doit deshonerer.

67    Une maniere de gens sont qu'il covient honerer par fine
      forche, et une autre c'on laist legierement passer; et par
      vive raison le vos mosterrai.

68    Sachiés par bone verité que se li sires de ceste vile ou
      aucuns haus hom, qui aucune bonté ou aucune amor
      m'aroit faite, sachiés en verité que ençois me greveroie
      ge moult que bel ostel et bon ne li fesisse.

59 Know truly that the right hand signifies our Lord and his glory, and the left the temptations of the world, of which there are many and enough.

60 Sweet Mary Magdalene gave alms according to God; she did not give according to the world, and know that she has her reward up in paradise.

61 "Many sins are forgiven her, because she hath much loved."

62 And our Lord said to Mary Magdalene, "Thy sins are forgiven thee."

63 Good gentlefolk, she truly repented and died a good death, and because of this our Lord crowned her in paradise together with his apostles and with his good company, and the scriptures tell us that she is the apostle of the apostles.

64 Good gentlefolk, now let us pray to our Lord that in his great pity and mercy he grant us a good death when we are truly repentant and truly confess our sins.

65 Good gentlefolk, listen carefully to this saying, "Tribute, to whom tribute is due . . . honor, to whom honor"; this is what the wise man says.

66 The wise man says that one should be careful whom one honors and whom one should not honor.

67 There is one kind of person whom you should honor absolutely, and another you should grant little honor: by means of lively reason I will show you.

68 You may be sure that if the lord of this town or some other notable has done me good or shown me consideration, I should be very sorry not to offer him good lodging and treat him well.

69 Et s'il n'avoit riens fait por moi, tant li devroie ie plus
tost faire; que ge le vous monsterrai.

70 Bontés, fait li sages, autre espiant et cele s'apert.

71 Et sachiés entierement que tex homme ou tele fame me
porroit bien venir que ge li torneroie l'oreille.

72 Tout ausi est-il orendroit.

73 La mere dieu sainte Marie d'Amiens, ele est votre dame
seur totes dames; c'est la dame du monde, c'est la roine
des glorieus chieus; c'est l'avoirs as pecheeurs et as
pecheris; ce est la sauveresse des ames; ce est espouse
nostre segneur; ele est mere Ihesu Crist; ele est temples
du saint esperit.

74 Ceste dame rapele les foliaus; ele redreche les cheus;
ceste dame, c'est secours as caïtis.

75 Ele conforte les dolereus; ele relieve les foibles; ele prie
pour le puile; ele maintient les honteus; elle deffent les
fames.

76 Sachiés bien, maus entra el monde par fame, et bien
revint el monde par fame.

77 La reproce que Eve conquist à fame leur toli Virgo
Maria, *quia quem celi capere non poterant, tuo gremio
contulisti.*

78 Ceste dame, ele est si haute et tant a de poisanche que
ele conprist en son ventre ce que chieus ne terre ne peut
comprendre: ce fu nostre segneur Ihesu Crist, que de
cele eure soions nous hui repairié à sainte eglise; que ce
soit au pourfit de nos cors et à la sauveté de nos ames!

69     And even if he had not done anything for me, I should still treat him this way, as I shall now explain.

70     Goodness, says the wise man, as this one looks, that one reveals.

71     And you should know that I might well turn my ear to some man or to some woman who came my way.

72     Now that's the way it all is.

73     The Mother of God, Saint Mary of Amiens, is your lady of all ladies; she is the lady of the world, she is the queen of the glorious heavens, she is the treasure of sinners, she is the savior of souls, she is the spouse of our Lord, she is the mother of Jesus Christ, she is the temple of the Holy Spirit.

74     This Lady calls back to her those who have strayed, she sets the fallen on their feet, she is rescue to the captives.

75     She comforts the sad, she strengthens the weak, she prays for the people, she sustains the despised, she guards women.

76     Remember that sin entered the world through woman and that good is brought back to the world through woman.

77     The reproach that Eve brought to woman was removed by the Virgin Mary, "since he whom the heavens could not contain, you have contained in your womb."

78     This Lady is so lofty and of such power that she conceived in her womb what neither heavens nor earth could conceive: our Lord Jesus Christ; and for that good fortune let us gather on this day in the holy church, to the profit of our bodies and the salvation of our souls!

*Descriptio sancti Geroimini* [added in red in margin]

79 Or entendés, bele douce gent. Pechierres, fait sains
[Gregoires *deleted*] Geroimes, fai la volenté à cele dame
qui est plaine de grant amor et de grant misericorde,
qu'il n'est cuers d'ome qui le peust penser, ne bouche
qui le peust dire, ne langue qui le seust descrire. *Et
iterum:* il n'est el monde pechierres ne pecheresse, tant
peust pechier, se tant avoit de vertu en soi qu'il peust
venir à sainte confession et à sainte repentance et à penitance, que la mere dieu sainte Marie n'ait greigneur
poisance de pardoner.

80 Ge le vous monstre: *Velle eius, velle dei; nolle eius, nolle
sui.*

81 L'escriture dist que quanque la mere dieu veult, il veult,
et quanque ele ne veult, il ne veult, il n'en a cure.

*De Theophile* [added in red in main text]

82 Nous trouvons en l'Escriture du clerc Theophile de
Rome, qu'il avoit dieu renoié de tot en tout, et avoit
pris du sanc de son front et en fist I cirografe, en despit
de dieu et du saint baptesme qu'il avoit recheu, et estoit
du tout devenus home au diable, dont dieu nous gart!

83 VII ans fu en tel pechié, ne ia ne vousist oïr de dieu
parler, et tant au chiés de VII ans, I samedi passa par
devant Sainte Marie la Reonde et oï c'on avoit com-
menchié le glorieus service de la glorieuse mere dieu
sainte Marie: *Salve sancta parens, enixa puerpera regem
et cetera.*

## The Description of Saint Jerome

79    Now listen, good gentlefolk. Sinners, Saint [Gregory—
      *deleted*] Jerome says, obey the will of this Lady who is
      full of great love and great mercy that no heart of man
      can conceive, nor mouth can speak, nor tongue can de-
      scribe, and he also says: "No sinner in the world, man
      or woman, can sin so much that if he had enough virtue
      in himself to come to holy confession and to holy repen-
      tance, the Mother of God Saint Mary would not have
      greater power to pardon."

80    I will show it to you: *Velle ejus, velle Dei; nolle ejus, nolle
      sui.*

81    For the scriptures say that whatever Holy Mary, Mother
      of God, wishes, he [Jesus] wishes; and whatever she
      does not wish, he does not wish or care for.

### About Theophilus

82    We read in the scriptures of the clerk Theophilus of
      Rome, who had denied God entirely and had taken
      the blood of his brow and made a chirograph counter
      to God and to holy baptism which he had received,
      and had completely become the devil's man, from
      which God save us!

83    For seven years he was in such sin that he could not
      bear to hear the name of God, and after seven years,
      when passing one Saturday in front of the church of
      Santa Maria Rotunda [the Pantheon], he heard that
      the glorious service of the glorious Mother of God had
      begun, "Hail, Holy Mary, who gave birth to the King!"

84    Quant li clers Theofiles oï et escouta la douce chanson
de la mere dieu sainte Marie, si li mua li sans, et se li
remua ses corages: A! Sainte Marie, fist-il, ià ne vous
renoiai ge onques, bele douce mere dieu; [f. 133v] or
priés à vo beneoit chier fil qu'il me pardoinst ce que
ge li ai mesfait.

85    Saciés entierement que por la bone repentance que li
clercs eut, la douce mere dieu sainte Marie commanda
[nostre segneur dieu *redundant*] au diable qu'il li rapor-
tast tost ariere le cirografe qu'il avoit escrit du sanc de
son front.

86    Sachiés li diables ne fu onques tant hardis qu'il le
retenist, ains le raporta à la douce mere dieu sainte
Marie, et la dame le rendi au clerc son sirografe, et li
clers servi la mere diu totes sa vie; et sachiés bien que
bon guerredon l'en rendi la dame, qu'il en est coronés
en la gloire de paradis avec la bele compaignie nostre
segneur. Prions nostre segneur tout ensemble c'à bone
fin nous atraie.

87    Bele douce gent, la mere diu sainte Marie d'Amiens
vous aporte pardon, parfoi voirement perdu, à ceus
et à celes qui pardon croient; car à chiaus et à celes
qui pardon ne croient certes ge n'en aport point, ne
iour ne demi; à chieus et à celes tout avant aporte ge
pardon qui croient el beneoit sacrement de sainte eglise.

88    Et cil et celes qui croient fermement que sainte confessions soit si haute chose et si disne, que si tost comme li
pechierres de bon cuer regehist son pechié à bouche de
prouvoire, et il en prent sainte penitance, que li diables
de son escrit l'efface, par la vertu de sainte confession;

84    When the clerk Theophilus heard and listened to the
      sweet song of the Mother of God, Saint Mary, his blood
      was moved and his heart was turned. "Ah! Holy Mary,"
      he said, "would I had not denied you, good, sweet
      Mother of God; now pray to your blessed, dear son
      that he pardon my crimes."

85    You may be sure that since the clerk had truly repented,
      the sweet Mother of God, Holy Mary, commanded the
      devil to bring immediately the chirograph which he
      [the clerk] had written with the blood of his forehead.

86    Know that the devil was not bold enough to hold on
      to it, and so he brought it back to the sweet Mother of
      God, Holy Mary, and the Lady gave the chirograph
      back to the clerk, and the clerk served the Lady as long
      as he lived; and know that he was well rewarded by
      her, for he is crowned in the glory of paradise in the
      good company of our Lord. Let us pray together to
      our Lord that he give us a good ending.

87    Good gentlefolk, the Mother of God, Saint Mary of
      Amiens, brings you pardon, which may be sometimes
      truly lost, to those men and women who believe in
      pardon. For those men and women who do not believe
      in pardon I bring none, not even a day or half a day;
      but to all believers in the blessed sacrament of the
      church I bring pardon.

88    And the men and women who firmly believe that holy
      confession is so lofty a thing and so worthy that when
      the sinner sincerely confesses his sin to the priest, and
      accepts the penance imposed on him, his name is blotted
      out from the devil's book by virtue of holy confession,

à chieus aporte ge pardon qui croient que dieu nostre
segneur soit ausi poissans de pardoner et tant ait en lui
de debonaireté comme il iert au ior et à l'eure qu'il fist
à saint Pierre pardon, qui trois fois le renoia, et le che-
valier qui le costé li entama, et le larron qui à sa destre
pendi, et la Madeleine qui moult estoit pecheresse;
sachiés qu'ele crei bien en pardon, si l'eut; sains Pierres
qui crei bien en pardon, si l'eut; et li chevaliers qui le
costé li entama, qui crei bien pardon, si l'eut; et li lerres
qui à la destre nostre segneur pendi crei bien pardon,
si l'eut.

89 Aprés de Cain qui ne crei pas pardon, si n'en ot point,
et sachiés Judas ne veust croire pardon si n'en ot point,
et si vous di en verité que li mauvais lerres qui pendi
à la senestre partie de nostre segneur il ne crei n'oient
en pardon, ne point n'en ot, dont il avint que l'ame de
lui en ala plus tost en enfer que l'ame de Judas qui deu
traï; et saciés par bone verité que l'ame du bon larron,
pour ce qu'il crei en pardon fu plus tost en paradis que
l'ame saint Pierre l'apostre. Or proiés nostre segneur
que vrai pardon puissons nous rechevoir.

90 Or entendés que dieu vous entende, un commandement
vous fas seur quanque vous tenés de dieu et seur le peril
de vos ames; et ge vous di vraiement que se vous le
faites, biens et profis vous en venra as ames de vous
et as cors.

to those I bring pardon, they who believe that our Lord God is powerful enough and good enough to forgive just as he did on the day and at the hour that he forgave Saint Peter, who denied him three times, and the soldier who pierced his side and the thief who was hanged at his right and that great sinner Mary Magdalene, who was granted pardon because she believed. Saint Peter, believing in pardon, received it; and the soldier who pierced his side and believed in pardon received it; and the thief hanging to the right of Christ believed in pardon and received it.

89   Then there is Cain, who did not believe in pardon and did not receive it at all, and Judas, who did not want to believe in pardon and did not receive it, and in truth the wicked thief who hung at the left side of Christ did not believe in or receive pardon, so that his soul went more quickly to hell than did the soul of Judas, who betrayed God. But know in truth that because the good thief believed in pardon, his soul came to paradise sooner than that of Peter the apostle. So pray to our Lord that we may receive true pardon.

90   Now, listen—so that the Lord will listen to you—to my commandment that applies to whatever you hold from the Lord, and to your very own souls, and I tell you truly that if you obey, you will benefit both in soul and in body.

91 Saciés que le requeste que ge vous ai faite, s'est tele com ge vous dirai; ge vous di que pour aumosnes que vous doigniés, ne pour penitanche que vous faciez, ne pour pardon que vous veigne, ne laissiés I seur ior de pardon à prendre.

92 Que si m'ait la glorieuse mere dieu. I iors venra que se vous en poiiés avoir I seul ior de pardon pour plain I autrestel mostier de fin or esmere volentiers le prendriés si m'aït dieu.

93 Sachiés certainement pour I pechié mortel VII ans de peneance, pour II, XIIII ans, pour IIII pechiés morteus XXVIII ans.

94 Saciés vraiement que ia ni faura ne ior ne eure que toute ne le fachiés ou en cest siecle ou en l'autre.

95 Bele douce gent, quant vous alés à confessé une seule fois en l'an, comment vous confessés vous, que dites-vous?

96 Sire, ie ai menti, ge ai iuré; si daubes vos pechiés, si m'aït Dieu et sa douce mere.

97 Li paignierres ne blanchist pas mex s'image, quant il le velt paindre que vous blanchisiés vos pechiés et vous escuses d'autruis pechiés.

98 Vous ne dites ore mie *quo loco, quo tempore;* vous ne dites pas quantes fois vous avés fait le pechié, n'à quele persone, n'à quele eure, [f. 134] ne en quel lieu vous fesites le pechié.

91   Know that the order I have given you is as I shall tell
     you: leave not a single day of pardon unclaimed, whether
     for the alms you may give, or penance you may do, or
     the pardon you may be granted.

92   May the glorious Mother of God help me! The day will
     come when if you could have a single day of pardon for
     a church as big [as this one] full of fine, pure gold you
     would gladly take it, so help me God!

93   You should know for certain that for one mortal sin
     [you must do] seven years of penance; for two, fourteen
     years; for four mortal sins, twenty-eight years.

94   Know truly that there will be neither day nor hour
     when you will not do [this penance], whether in this
     world or the next.

95   Good gentlefolk, when you go to confess only once a
     year, how do you confess; what do you say?

96   Lord, I have lied, I have cursed: you so whiten your sins,
     may God and his sweet mother help me!

97   The painter whitens the image that he paints just as
     much as you whiten your sins and overlook the sins
     of others.

98   You never say *quo loco, quo tempore;* you do not say
     how many times you have sinned, against what person,
     at what time or in what place you committed the sin.

99  Certes plus seroit li pechiés lais en cest moustier que la
aval en mi ces chans, pour tant seulement que la terre
est benoite; plus seroit luxure vilaine d'un prestre ou
d'un home marié, que d'un garchon ou d'une garche.

100 Car sachiés vraiement quiconques depieche ne deront
mariage il deront et depiece la bele char nostre segneur,
il desment le saint sacrement nostre segneur, il desdit
et deffait la sainte escriture et le saintes paroles nostre
segneur.

101 Or prions nostre segneur Ihesu Crist que en ferme foi
et en ferme creance nous tiegne.

102 Bele douce gent, li apostres se nous ensaigne que nus
ne doit metre s'entente en une chose, seulement en
dieu servir, mais en toutes manieres de bones weures,
en iuner, en veillier, en ourer, en faire peneanche,
en porter haire, en pardon prendre.

103 Entendés bien ceste parole; legierement parlerai à
vous; ge vous di loiaument par doner a on pardon et
par pardon a on dieu. Or ia aucuns caitis qui dient: Par
les ex bieu! cil cil *[sic]* clerc, cil prestre nous font erbe
paistre, s'il welent!

104 Par la teste bieu! pardons c'on vent n'est pas drois pardons. Il mentent comme mauvais bougre, desloial larron
qu'il sunt.

105 Que nous trovons que quant nostre segneur dieu aloit
par terre, il trova monsegneur Saint Pierre et monsegneur Saint Andrieus, frere estoient et pescheeur de
possons; à nostre segneur pleut qu'il ne prisent riens
de poisson là où il getoient leur rois, ne dechà ne delà,
et nostre segneur savoit bien la u li poisson estoient.

99　Indeed, your sins will be uglier in this church than out there in the fields, simply because this is consecrated ground; lust is uglier in a priest or a married man than in a boy or a girl.

100　For you should know that whoever destroys and breaks up marriage tears up and destroys the good flesh of our Lord; he denies the holy sacrament; he violates the holy scripture and the holy words of our Lord.

101　Now let us pray to our Lord Jesus Christ that he keep us firm in faith and belief.

102　Good gentlefolk, the apostle teaches us that nobody should agree to anything other than to serve God in every kind of good work: in fasting and in vigils; in praying and in doing penance; in wearing the hair shirt and in asking pardon.

103　Listen carefully; I shall speak gently to you: I tell you that by giving you are pardoned, and by pardon you have God. Now there are some wretches who say, "By the eyes of Dog! These clerics, these priests can have us graze the pasture, if they so want!"

104　"By the head of Dog! Pardons sold are not true pardons; they lie like the bad buggers, the treacherous thieves they are."

105　We find, then, that when our Lord was on earth, he found my lord Saint Peter and my lord Saint Andrew, who were brothers and fishermen, and it pleased our Lord that they should take no fish there where they threw their net, not this way or that, and our Lord knew exactly where the fish were.

106 Segneurs, dist nostre segneur getés vos rois par dechà,
s'arés asés du poisson, et il si firent, si en prirent à si très
grant plenté, que poi s'en fali qu'il n'afonderent.

107 Adonc s'aperchurent li doi preudome que ce estoit li
vrais dieu.

108 Ha! sire, firent il, souffrés nous que nous alons en vostre
compaignie, que vous estes li vrais dieu.

109 Ge le vous octroi, dist nostre segneur; vous estiés pes-
cheor de poissons, mais ge vous ferai pescheors d'ames.

110 Bele douce gent, saciés qu'il laissierent entierement
quanque il avoient et vert et sec, pour avoir pardon;
il furent apostres nostre segneur et prehechierent la foi
toute lor vie, et au deerrain il en furent pendu cascons
en une crois, Saint Pierre les piés contremont et le chief
contreval, et Saint Andrieus de travers, et tout pour
avoir pardon.

111 Sains Bertremex en fu escorchiés tous vis; Saint Lorens
en fu grilliés et rostis tous vis, et tout pour avoir pardon;
Saint Ipolites en fu detrais à IIII chevaus sauvages en la
cité de Rome, et tout pour avoir pardon; Sainte Katerine
en fu enroée en une plaine de tranchans alemeles afilées;
Sainte Marguerite en fu decolée; Sainte Agnes [*recte*
Agatha] en eut ses beles mameles traités hors de son cors
à I tortoir de fer et tout pour avoir pardon et paradis.

112 Si m'aït dieu! Cil de Chistiaus, cil de Premonstere,
cil de Saint Beneoit, cil de Saint Augustin n'aront mie
le pardon de paradis pour noient; certes moult à envis
l'achateriees autrestant comme il font.

106 "Sirs," said our Lord, "throw your nets over there and you will have enough fish"; and they did it, and they took so much that they almost sank.

107 And then the two good men perceived that this was the true God.

108 "Ha! Lord," they said, "allow us to join your company— you are indeed the true God."

109 "This I grant you," said our Lord; "you were fishers of fish, but I shall make you fishers of souls."

110 Good gentlefolk, I want you to realize that these men gave up all that they had, both quick and dead, for pardon; they were our Lord's apostles and preached the faith all their lives, and in the end they were hanged on a cross, Saint Peter with his feet up and his head down and Saint Andrew diagonally—and all this to have pardon.

111 Saint Bartholomew was flayed alive; Saint Lawrence was grilled and roasted alive, and all to have pardon; Saint Hippolytus was torn apart by four wild horses in the city of Rome, and all to have pardon; Saint Catherine was tortured on a wheel full of sharp blades; Saint Margaret was beheaded; Saint Agnes [*recte* Agatha] had her lovely breasts torn from her body with iron tongs, and all in order to have pardon and paradise.

112 May God help me! The Cistercians, the Premonstratensians, the Benedictines, the Augustinians shall not have the pardon of paradise for nothing; no, indeed, given the purchasing that they do.

113    Que sachiés par bone foi que dès le iors de la Sainte
Crois dusc'au ior de Pasques ne mangeront il iamais
que tant ior tantes fois, ne iamais ne mengeront de char,
ne iamais ne gerront seur coute de plume, ne iamais
ne parleront se par congié non pour parent ne pour
ami qui les voise visiter; et se par aventure avenoit qu'il
trespasse I seul point du commandement de lor rieulle
et eust trespassé obedience, et avenist que il moreust
sans ce qu'il n'en eust esté à sainte confession et à sainte
repentance et à sainte peneance, et eust autrestant de
biens fais comme tout li saint de paradis, ge n'en don-
roie pas une pome porrie de ce qu'il ieust deservi les
paines et les tormens d'enfer, et tant comme dex seroit
dex, ne ià dex merci n'en aroit.

114    [f. 134v] Proions dieu nostre segneur Jhesu Crist que
des mortex paines d'enfer nous deffende par sa grant
pitié et par sa grant misericorde.

115    Bele douce gent, la mere dieu sainte Marie vous est
venue requerre à ceste sainte matinée; mais sachiés bien
que ce n'est pas pour besoig quele ait de vous mais pour
le grant besoig [qu'ele a de vous *deleted*] que vous avés
de li; car sachiés en verité que tout ausi comme il nous
est mestiers que li blé et les vignes et li bien terrien vont
renovelant d'an en an C^m tans et C^m tans et C^m tans vous
iert il graindes mestiers que li bien de sainte eglise et les
orisons et li saint sacrement nostre segneur vous renove-
lent cascun an as ames de vous; or proiés donques nostre
segneur Jhesu Christ que disnement le vous laist rechevoir par sa grant pitié et par sa grant misericorde.

113 Know in good faith that from the day of the Holy Cross to Easter day they eat only as many times as there are days; they never eat meat, they do not sleep on a down mattress, they never speak without leave, even if a relative or a friend visits, and if by chance [one of them] should break a single point of the commandment of their rule and should break his obedience, and if he should happen to die without having been to holy confession and holy repentance and holy penance, and had done as much good as all the saints in paradise, I would not give a rotten apple that he had [not] deserved the pains and torments of hell, and as long as God is God, he will not have God's mercy.

114 Let us pray God that our Lord Jesus Christ save us with his great pity and his great mercy from the mortal pains of hell.

115 Good gentlefolk, the Mother of God, Saint Mary, has called for your help on this holy morning, not because she needs you but because of the great need you have of her; for know in truth that just as it's essential for us that wheat and vines and the fruits of the earth be renewed year by year, it is a hundred thousand times, a hundred thousand times, a hundred thousand times [more] essential that your souls be renewed every year by the goodness of the holy church and the prayers and the holy sacrament of our Lord; now pray to our Lord Jesus Christ that he allow you to receive it worthily, through his great pity and his great mercy.

*De sancto Matheo* [in red; inserted in line break]

116 Bele douce gent, Saint Mahius nous raconte par le sainte
evangile que nostre segneur aloit I ior en la terre d'outre-
mer avec ses apostres et sachiés moult le sievoient grant
plenté de gent de moult de manieres et de diverses pensées.

117 L'une maniere de gent sievoient nostre segneur pour
le grant plenté de mengier qu'il avoient aveques lui.

118 Le seconde maniere de gent qui le sievoient, c'estoit
pour les beles miracles qu'il faisoit; car il faisoit mors
resuciter, il faisoit mesiaus monder, il faisoit contrais
redrechier, il faisoit avules veoir, il faisoit muiaus parler,
il faisoit les sours oïr; saciés par bone verité que de
toutes les maladies, tout à I mot, que cuers d'ome peust
[veoir *deleted*] penser ne ex veoir, quiconques le requeroit
de cuer vrai, tous et totes les garissoit.

119 La tierche maniere de gent qui nostre segneur sievoient
c'estoit pour savoir s'il le peussent reprendre en aucune
maniere, mais il ne le savoient de coi reprendre.

120 Si trouvons que nostre segneur dieu demanda à ses
deciples: Segneurs, ceste gent qui chi me sievent, que
dient il de moi, que ge sui?

121 Et il respondirent à nostre segneur: Certes, Sire, il
dient tex ia que Jehans Baptistres est dex; li autres dient
que Elies li profetes est dex, li tiers dient que Geremies
li prophete est dex. Et nostre segneur leur respondi
adonques: Ore, segneurs, et vous qui vées et oés mes
weures et mes fais et mes paroles plus souvent qu'il
ne font, qui creés vous qui ge sui? qu'en dites-vous?
*Respondens, Simon Petrus dixit.* Et sans doute Saint

### From Saint Matthew

116 Good gentlefolk, Saint Matthew tells us in the Holy Gospel that our Lord once went abroad with his apostles, and know that many people followed him— people of all kinds and different ways of thinking.

117 Some people followed our Lord because of the plentiful food they had with him.

118 Others followed him for his wonderful miracles; for he brought the dead back to life, he cleansed lepers, he caused cripples to walk, he enabled the blind to see, the mute to speak, and the deaf to hear; I tell you truly that he instantly healed anyone who sincerely beseeched him, man or woman, of every disease your mind can conceive of or your eyes can see.

119 The third kind of person who followed Christ were those who sought to find fault with him, but they found no such cause.

120 And we find that our Lord God asked his disciples, "Sirs, these people who follow me, who do they say I am?"

121 And they answered our Lord, "Indeed, Lord, some say John Baptist is God; others say Elias the prophet is God; a third group, that Jeremiah the prophet is God." And our Lord then answered: "Now, Sirs, you who have seen and heard my works and my deeds and my words more often than them, who do you think I am? What do you say?"—*Respondens, Simon Petrus dixit.* And doubtless

Pierre qui estoit plus agus en la reanche que tout li
autre, respondi en tele maniere: En non dieu, segneur,
fist Saint Pierre, ge ne sai que li autre diront, mais en-
droit moi, en dirai ma pensée. Ge di que vous estes li
vrais dieu qui vit et regne sans fin et sans commenche-
ment ne iamais vos pooirs [names *deleted*] n'amenuisera.

122 Et nostre segneur respondi adonques: *Beatus es, Simon
Bariona quia caro et sanguis non revelavit tibi sed pater
meus qui est in celis; et ego dico tibi quia tu es Petrus et
super hanc petram edificabo ecclesiam meam et porte inferi
non prevalebunt adversus eum* [*recte* eam], *et tibi dabo
claves regni celorum et quoque* [*recte* quodcumque]
*solveris super terram erit solutum et in celis, et quoque*
[*recte* quodcumque] *ligaveris super terram erit ligatum
in celis et cetera.*

123 Bele douce gent, or ne dist pas nostre segneur, Pierre,
beneois soies tu, ains li dist; Pierre, tu es beneios, que
tes sans ne ta char n'as pas revelé en toi, ne le ne t'a pas
issi apris à parler, mais mes peres qui est es chieus en sa
gloire la sus amont; et ge te di que tu es Pierre et seur
ceste pierre edefierai ge me eglise. Biaus amis, veus-tu
savoir porquoi il parla en tele maniere nostre segneur?

124 Mesire Saint Pierre si est fers en foi; et vous savés bien
que pierre est la plus [f. 135] ferme chose qui soit; autant
vaut pierres comme fers en creance; et pour ce li dist il
nostre segneur, qu'il edifieroit seur cele pierre s'eglise:
Pierres, dist nostre segneur, ge te donrai les clés de
paradis et du regne du chiel là sus amont.

Saint Peter, who was more intelligent than all the others, answered in this way: "In the name of God," said Saint Peter, "I do not know what the others will say, but as for me, I shall say what I think; I say that you are the true God who lives and reigns without end and without beginning, and never will your power wane."

122    And our Lord answered him as follows: *Beatus es, Simon Bariona quia caro et sanguis non revelavit tibi sed pater meus qui est in celis; et ego dico tibi quia tu es Petrus et super hanc petram edificabo ecclesiam meam et porte inferi non prevalebunt adversus eam, et tibi dabo claves regni celorum et quodcumque solveris super terram erit solutum et in celis, et quodcumque ligaveris super terram erit ligatum in celis,* etc.

123    Good gentlefolk, now our Lord did not say, "Bless you, Peter"; he said, "Peter, you are blessed, since it was not your blood and your flesh that told you this, for they have not taught you to speak, but my Father who is in heaven in his lofty glory; and I say to you that you are Peter, and upon this rock I shall build my church." Good friend, do you want to know why our Lord spoke in this way?

124    The faith of my lord Saint Peter is as strong as iron. You know that there is nothing stronger than stone; we believe that stone is equal to iron, and it was because of this that our Lord said that he would build his church upon that rock. "Peter," said our Lord, "I shall give you the keys of paradise and the kingdom of heaven above."

125 Pierre, fist nostre segneur, quanque tu loieras en terre
ier loié et confermé es chieus, et quanque tu asouras en
terre iert asous et confirmé es chieus la sus amont.

126 Pierres, dist nostre segneur, ie te doins poesté es chiaus
et en terre de loier et de desloier et d'escommenier et
d'asourre; quanque tu escommenieras en terre, iert
escommenié es chieus là sus, et quanque tu assourras
en terre sera asous es chieus là sus amont.

127 Bele douce gent, ce deservi il por ce qu'il fu de ferme
creanche: proiés dieu qu'en ferme creance nous tiegne.

128 Bele douce gent, autrestele poesté et autretele digneté
comme nostre segneur Saint Pierre eut en terre, a ore
li apostoles de Rome, et ausi grant poesté et ausi grant
digneté a I archevesques en s'archevesquié; *descendendo,*
et autant I evesques en s'evesquié et I prestres en sa
paroise.

129 Que sachiés les baillies ne sont pas donées oelment, ains
vont de degré en degré en deschendant; mais sachiés
entierement que toutes les confessions que vous dites
à votre segneur de prestre, vos les dites à la bele bouche
nostre segneur Dex l'otroie et conferme en paradis.

130 Or prions nostre segneur dieu Ihesu Crist et sa douce
mere que vraie confession nous atraie.

131 Bele douce gent, vous poés hui faire le plus haute iornée
et le mieudre et le plus bele que vous onques feissiés, se
pechiés ou envie ou avarisses, ou diables ne le vous toust.

125     "Peter," said our Lord, "that which you bind on earth will be bound and confirmed in heaven, and whoever you absolve on earth will be absolved and confirmed in heaven."

126     "Peter," said our Lord, "I grant you power in heaven and on earth to bind and to unbind, to excommunicate and to absolve; whosoever you excommunicate on earth shall be excommunicated up in heaven, and whosoever you absolve on earth shall be absolved up in heaven."

127     Good gentlefolk, Peter deserved this since his faith was firm; pray God that he hold us in firm faith.

128     Good gentlefolk, whatever power and whatever dignity our lord Saint Peter had on earth is now held by the pope in Rome. The archbishop in the archdiocese also has the same power, and, coming down the scale, so has a bishop in his diocese and a priest in his parish.

129     You should know that charges are not assigned equally, and so they go from step to step in descending order, but know that all confessions that you make to your lord the priest are said to our Lord God; may he grant and confirm them in paradise.

130     Now let us pray to our Lord God, Jesus Christ, and his sweet mother that he will bring us to confess our sins sincerely.

131     Good gentlefolk, today you can have the highest and the best and the most beautiful day you have ever had, if sins or envy or greed or the devil do not prevent it.

132 Que sachiés entierement que dès icele eure que li premiers quarriaus de ceste eglise fu asis et li premiers enfes i fu baptisés et regenerés en sains fons et li premiers entendemens et li premiers sacremens nostre segneur i fu celebrés, se dieu ait part en l'ame de moi! li diables li anemis ne fu si tormentés comme il iert au ior d'ui.

133 Et savés vous pourcoi il si tormentés iert? Si me face dieu pardon! que ce est pour les haus pardons et pour les hautes orisons que on vous aporte entre vous bons crestiens, qui bien crées en pardons.

134 Bele douce gent, à vous tous ensanle et à cascun par soi qui vourés reconnoistre la mere dieu Sainte Marie d'Amiens, qui est votre mere eglise, dont li bien vous vienent; car il vous envient ole, cresme, baptesme, enoliement, enterrement, noches, mariages, li beneois sacremens en est fais en sainte eglise.

135 Li sires li evesques d'Amiens qui est nostre pere espiritueus est tenus à vous conduire et mener en paradis, en la benoite compaignie d'angles, d'arcangles, de martirs, de confès et de benes eureuses virges qui ont deservi le regne de paradis par martire de lor cors et par espandemens de lor sanc.

136 Sachiés vraiement à tous les biensfaiteus de la glise me dame Sainte Marie d'Amiens envoie [XXVII *deleted*] VII$^{xx}$ iors de vrai pardon à alegier les vies peneanches que vous devés faire ens el cruel fu de purgatoire.

137 Dont mesire Saint Augustin nous dist par cest parole: *Sola dies purgatorium super omnes sanctorum omnium.*

132 For know well that from the very hour that the first squared stone of this church was laid and the first children were baptized and reborn in the holy fonts and the first offices and sacraments of our Lord were celebrated here—God save my soul!—our enemy the devil was never so tormented as he will be today.

133 And do you know why he will be so tormented? May God pardon me! It is because of the lofty pardons and the lofty prayers brought to you good Christians, who believe in pardons.

134 Good gentlefolk, all of you together and each of you individually who recognize the Mother of God, Saint Mary of Amiens, which is your mother church, from which good comes, for to you come oil, chrism, baptism, extreme unction, burial, betrothal, marriage, [and] the blessed sacraments made in the holy church.

135 Our spiritual father, the lord bishop of Amiens, is duty-bound to conduct and lead you to paradise in the blessed company of angels, archangels, martyrs, confessors, and good and blessed virgins who have earned the kingdom of heaven through martyrdom and the shedding of their blood.

136 Know truly that to all the benefactors of the church my Lady, Saint Mary of Amiens, sends 140 days of true pardon to mitigate the vivid penance that you must do in the cruel fire of purgatory.

137 Of which my lord Saint Augustine said these words: *Sola dies purgatorium super omnes sanctorum omnium.*

138   Qui prendroit, fait Saint Augustin, le plus tenre pucele
      qui onques fust née de ventre de fame, et fust escorchiée
      toute vive, comme Saint Bertremex, et ne peust morir, et
      si fust la pucele *[illegible deletion]* enroée comme Sainte
      Katerite, et ne peust morir; et fust bolie en oile boulant,
      comme Saint Jehans li euvangeliste, et ne peust morir; et
      eust torses les mameles hors du cors, et ne peust morir,
      comme eut la damoisele Sainte Agates: sachiés [f. 135v]
      entierement que se tout cil torment li avenoient et asés
      autre torment que bien nomeroie, se ie voloie, estoient
      I seus tormens, et les esteust soufrir à cele damoisele C
      ans et tous les iors des C ans les sentist et ne peust morir
      la pucele, ne li feroient il tant de mal comme feroit I
      seus iors del cruel fu de purgatoire.

139   Et saciés que ge vous proverai par vive raison pourcoi li
      feus de purgatoire est apelés purgatoire: pour ce que les
      ames as bons amis nostre segneur i sont espurgiés.

140   Que sachiés par bone verité que tant comme i convenra
      estre les ames qui dedens entroient qu'eles seront si
      espurgiés, qu'eles seront si netes comme clers solaus,
      si clers comme est la lune et li solaus.

141   Dont Saint Gregoire nous tesmoigne en cel maniere:
      Escrisiés, fait Saint Gregoire, I fu de vermeilles couleurs
      en cele maniere, et faites I fu de vers espines d'autre
      part; sachiés que c'est li plus crueus fus qui soit et li plus
      destrois en terre, que d'espines; sachiés que dex nous
      tesmoigne et l'escriture par la bouche monseigneur

138    "Take, for example," said Saint Augustine, "the most tender virgin who was ever born of the womb of woman, and [imagine that] she was flayed alive, like Saint Bartholomew, and could not die; and if this virgin were racked on the wheel like Saint Catherine and could not die; and if she were boiled in boiling oil like Saint John the Evangelist and could not die; and if she had the breasts torn from her body and could not die, like the damsel Saint Agatha: be sure that if all this torment came to her, and much other torment that I could mention, if I wished, [to make] one sole torment, and if this damsel were to suffer it for a hundred years and every day of the hundred years [remained] unable to die, it would not cause her as much pain as one single day of the cruel fire of purgatory."

139    And know that I shall prove through lively reason why the fire of purgatory is called purgatory: it is because the souls of the good friends of our Lord are purged there.

140    And know in good truth that as much as it is appropriate that the souls enter into purgatory, it is equally appropriate that they be so purged that they shall be as clean as the bright sun, as bright as the moon and the sun.

141    Of which Saint Gregory bears witness in this manner: "Take note," said Saint Gregory, "of a fire of red color in this fashion, and make a fire of green thorns on the other hand; know that this—the fire of thorns—is the cruelest fire that exists, and the most rigorous on earth." Know that God and the scriptures witness by the mouth

Saint Gregoire, que ne plus de force ne d'ardure que ara li fus qui iert portrais et pains à la maisiere aroit contre le fu que vous ariés enbrasé et espris; noient plus n'aroit li grans fus terriens de vertu contre le grant fu du purgatoire.

142 Et se vous demandés: Maistre, combien convenra il ces ames estre dedens ces grans tourmens de purgatoire qui si sont cruel?

143 Si m'aït nostre segneur! Bele douce gent, sachiés en verité selonc ce que li pechieres ou la pecheresse aront meffait, li un plus que li autre, li un X ans, li autres XX ans, LX ans, C, CC, III$^c$, V$^c$, M, II$^m$.

144 Si m'aït nostre segneur! Bele gent, ià iors ne eure n'en faura que vous n'en faciés la peneance, selonc ce que vous faites les pechiés; car sachiés c'on ne vous garche mie le centisme partie de peneance c'on deveroit.

145 Que sachés bien que tout ausi comme li segneur terrien ont asises lor iustices seur les homes terriens de lor meffais, qu'il font li I gregneur que li autre selonc ce qu'il ont deservi sunt iugié en terre; ausi vous di ge, li segneur terrien ont poesté seur lor homes de metre en prison, s'il welent, et de desmembrer s'il vuelent.

146 Sachiés, il ont poesté seur les cors, mais il mie poesté seur les ames.

147 Bele douce gent, vous poés veoir, plus fort nostre segneur a peoir seur les cors et seur les ames; bien a peoir nostre segneur de vous envoier une si tres dolereuse fievre s'il velt, ou une si très dolereuse *[illegible deletion]* goute, ou I si grant mehaig que iamais delivré n'en serés, s'il n'en a merci.

of Saint Gregory that there is no force and no burning
worse than the fire that was portrayed and painted on
the wall as against the fire that will have set you ablaze
and burned you, nor do the great fires on earth have
any strength against the great fire of purgatory.

142 And you may ask, Master, how long should these souls
be in these great torments of purgatory that are so cruel?

143 May our Lord help me! Good gentlefolk, know in truth
that the sinner will be punished according to the evil
he or she has done: some for ten years; others for twenty
years; still others for sixty years, or for a hundred, two
hundred, three hundred, five hundred, one thousand,
two thousand years.

144 May our Lord help me! Good people, there will be
neither day nor hour when you will not do the penance
appropriate for your sins, for you are not called upon
to perform as much as a hundredth part of the penance
that you have incurred.

145 And know well that just as the earthly lords hold rights
of justice over earthly men for their crimes and impose
penalties of different magnitudes, according to how
they are judged on earth, so, I tell you, earthly lords
have power over their men to put them in prison,
if they wish, and to dismember them, if they wish.

146 Yet having power over their bodies, they have no power
over their souls.

147 Good gentlefolk, you can see that our Lord has greater
power over bodies and souls; our Lord, has enough
power to send you a wretched fever, if he wishes, or
a very miserable gout, or such great suffering that
you will never be free of it unless he so wills.

148 Nostre segneur Ihesu Crist a asis ses asises à cascun pechié, selonc ce qu'il sont plus lait et plus vilain li un que li autre: por I pechié mortel VII ans de peneanche, et pour cascun pechié mortel VII ans; or regardés par quantes fois vous avés pechié.

149 Bele douce gent, si m'aït la mere dieu! que li prestre ne vous carchent c'un peu de peneance entre vous; qu'il si vous carchoient selonc vos meffais, il vous espeventeroient si que vous lairiés tout ester; mais mestiers vous est que vous fachiés aucune peneance.

150 Car sachiés quiconques est pris en peneance et en aucune confession et en vraie repentance, il ne puet estre damnés, qu'il ne voist faire sa peneance el fu de purgatoire; et puis que l'ame entre dedens ce fu, donques set ele bien qu'ele ne puet falir à le gloire de paradis.

151 Enon diu! donques puet ele bien dire une canchon que souventes fois ai öi chanter:

> Bone est la dolor
> Dont ge atent douchour
> Et soulas et ioie.

152 Beles douce gent, en ces gries tormens que ge vous ai devisés, sunt les ames de vos peres et de vos meres, sunt les ames de vos sereurs et de vos freres, sunt les ames de vos amis et de vos amies, qui hui en cest ior vous prient merci; et savés vous [f. 136] qu'eles dient? *Miseremini, miseremini mei, saltem vos amici mei, quia manus Domini tetigit me.*

148 Our Lord Jesus Christ has set a penalty for each sin, according to which is uglier and more foul than the other: for one mortal sin, seven years of penance, and the same for each mortal sin; now consider how many sins you have committed.

149 Good gentlefolk, may the Mother of God help me! May the priests impose only a slight penance on you, for if they sentenced you according to your crimes they would frighten you to death; but it is necessary that you do some penance.

150 For know anyone taken [by death] in a [state of] penitence and confession and true repentance cannot be damned if he is purged by the fires of purgatory, and after his soul enters that fire, it knows that it cannot fail to come to the glories of paradise.

151 By God, that's so! And the soul can then sing a song that I have often heard:

> Good is the suffering
> From which I await sweetness
> And solace and joy.

152 Good gentlefolk, in these great torments that I have described are the souls of your fathers and your mothers, the souls of your sisters and your brothers, the souls of your friends, men and women, who today are praying to you for pity; do you know what they are saying? "Have pity on me, have pity on me, at least you my friends, because the hand of the Lord hath touched me."

153  Hé! hé! mi ami, mes amies, mi fil, mes files, qui m'avés
fait perdre tantes messes, tantes matines, tant vespres,
tantes complies; tantes beles aumosnes ai laisiés à faire
et tant grant pardon *[illegible deletion]* à rechevoir, pour
vous norrir et por vous alever; por dieu, aiés merci de
moi; car la verge nostre segneur m'a touché.

154  Sachiés, bele douce gent, hui en cest ior, en ceste sainte
matinée, poés les ames de vos peres et de vos amis plus
liés et plus ioiaus faire que se vous leur doniés plain cest
moustier d'or; car, si m'envoit dieu pardon! il sevent
orendroit mex qu'est pardon et qu'il vaut que vous
ne savés.

155  De VII$^{xx}$ iornées vous poés hui aprochier plus près de
paradis que vous n'estiées ier matin, se pechiés ou envie
ou covoitise ne le vous toust, et autant as ames de vos
peres et de vos meres, et autant à toutes les ames que
vous meinés à compaignier.

156  Or prions nostre segneur Iesu Crist que disnement le
vous laist rechevoir par sa grant pitié et par sa grant
misericorde.

157  Beles douce gent, entendés bien ceste parole; legierement parlerai à vous.

158  Après vous envoie mesire li evesques pour le secors de
vos ames et de tous chiaus qui vous m'orrés acompai-
gnier, trestous les biensfais de sen evesquié; car saciés
que trestous les iors que li siecles duerra, n'ara leu ne
chanté messe, ne matines ne oroisons de sainte eglise,
que vous n'en soiés parchoner; et sachiés bien c'autel
compaignie et autel partie vous en otroient comme il
en atendent à rechevoir au grant ior del iuise.

153    Hey, hey! my friends, men and women, my sons, my daughters, you who have made me miss so many masses, so many matins, so many vespers, so many complines; I have failed to give so many good offerings of alms and missed receiving so many pardons in order to nourish and raise you; for God's sake have pity on me, for the rod of our Lord has struck me!

154    Know, good gentlefolk, on this very day and this holy morning, you can render the souls of your fathers and your friends happier and more joyous than if you gave them this church full of gold, for, may God pardon me, they now know better than you what pardon is and what it is worth!

155    You can today be 140 days nearer to paradise than you were yesterday morning—if sins or envy or covetousness do not cut you off from it—and so may the souls of your fathers and mothers, and of all others you pray for.

156    Now let us pray our Lord Jesus Christ that of his great pity and his great mercy he will allow you to worthily receive [this pardon].

157    Good gentlefolk, listen carefully to this word; I shall speak softly to you.

158    My lord the bishop, to save your souls and those of all with whom you wish to associate, will send you all the benefits of his diocese, for I tell you that until the end of time, no mass will be sung, or matins or prayers of the holy church, of which you are not part, and be assured that they will win for you such company and such a part as they hope to receive on the great day of judgment.

159   Or proions nostre segneur que disnement le vous laist
      rechevoir.

160   *Dignus est operarius mercede sua.*

161   Beles douce gent, sachiés quant uns bons serians a bien
      servi son seigneur tout l'an contreval et vient au chief
      de son terme, il est bien disnes d'avoir son loier et sa
      deserte.

162   Tout ausi est il ore; il est bien drois et raisons que entre
      vous qui vourés vostre mere eglise reconoistre et le glo-
      rieus pardon rechevoir et prendre; bien est drois que
      vous sachiés que le merite vous en devés avoir du
      rechevoir.

163   Saciés en l'evesquié d'Amiens a VII$^c$ et LX et XVII
      prestres; de cascun avés III messes estorées tous les
      ans que li siecles duerra: la premiere du Saint Esperit,
      la seconde de Nostre Dame Sainte Marie; et la tierche
      des beneois feeus nostre segneur dieu.

164   Proiés nostre segneur que vraiement le vous laist
      rechevoir.

165   Après il a en l'evesquié d'Amiens XXVI abeies et XXVI
      abés, que gris, que noirs, que blans nonains que noires;
      sachiés que noient plus que vous poés esrachier l'ongle
      de vo doit sans vous grever, il ne vous pueent geter hors
      de lor biens fais que iamais feront tant comme li siecles
      duerra, comme en poures sanuler, en poures couchier
      et lever, en poures recauchier et revestir, en lever as
      matines, en veillier, en ouorer, en iuner, et tous les biens
      tout à I mot que iamais feront, et en tous chiaus c'on
      fist puis cele eure que les abeies furent estorées, à tous
      chiaus qui lor aumosnes envoieront à lor mere eglise.

159    Now let us pray our Lord that he will allow you worthy
       receipt [of this pardon].

160    "For the laborer is worthy of his hire."

161    Good gentlefolk, know that when a good servant has
       served his lord well all through the year and comes to
       the end of his term, he is indeed worthy of his recom-
       pense and his reward.

162    That's exactly how it is now. It is right and proper that
       among yourselves you should want to recognize your
       mother church and receive and take the glorious par-
       don; it is right that you should know the good that
       this will have done you.

163    Know that in the diocese of Amiens there are 777 priests;
       from each you will have three masses said every year for
       all the years that time will last: one for the Holy Spirit,
       the second for Our Lady Saint Mary, and the third for
       the departed souls blessed by our Lord God.

164    Pray our Lord that he will truly allow you to receive
       [this pardon].

165    Then there are in the diocese of Amiens twenty-six
       abbeys and twenty-six abbots, both gray and black, as
       well as white nuns and black; no more could you pull
       out the nail of your finger without hurting yourself than
       they could cast you out from all the good deeds they will
       ever do till the end of time—such as caring for the poor,
       giving them a bed, shoes and clothes; such as getting
       up for matins and vigils, praying and fasting and all
       the good deeds, in a word, that they will ever do, and
       all they have done since the time when the abbeys were
       established—[in the name of] all those who shall send
       their offerings to their mother church.

166    Prions nostre segneur que benignement le vous laist
rechevoir.

167    Après il i a encore en l'evesquié XXX priortés dont
mesire li evesques vous a estoré I trentel à tous les iors
que li siecles duerra. Et savés vous que est trenteus? Ce
est de cascune priorté une messe estorée à tous les iors
que le siecles duerra pour tous les biens faiteurs de
l'eglise d'Amiens.

168    Proiés nostre segneur que vous le puissiés rechevoir.

169    Près, [f. 136v] beles douce gent, mesire li evesques vous
envoie le plus haut pardon qui onques vous fust envoiés;
car il vous envoie pardon et asolution de tous les seremens que vous onques iurastes fors II; les II seremens
savés quel i sont?

170    Sachiés se vous avés iuré serement por autrui catel tolir
et por sainte eglise amenuisier; sachiés que tel serement
ne vous aporté ge pas pardon; car sachiés ne archevesques ne vesques n'i a pooir. *Non dimittitur peccatum, nisi
restituatur ablatum.*

171    Que si m'aït Dex! Il ne dist pas le vraie escriture: se tu as
eu de l'autrui par male desraison, rendre le te convient;
et se tu as à autrui mauvais blasme alevé, si m'aït Dex!
tu n'en pues estre quites dusc'à cele eure que tu l'eraies
mis en tel point là u il estoient, et graignor paine vous
i covient metre à son bons les raquellir, que vous ne
fesistes au mauvais aquellir.

172    Car, à non diu, ensi le dist dex, ou rendre ou pendre à le
porte et au gibet d'enfer.

166    Pray our Lord that he allow you to favorably receive
       [this pardon].

167    Then there are also in the diocese [of Amiens] thirty
       priories in which my lord the bishop has established
       for you a trental each day that time lasts. And do you
       know what this trental is? There is in each priory a mass
       established every day for all the days that time endures
       for all the benefactors of the church of Amiens.

168    Pray our Lord that you may receive it.

169    Then, good gentlefolk, my lord the bishop sends you
       the highest pardon that was ever sent to you; for he
       sends pardon and absolution for all the oaths that you
       have ever sworn except two—do you know what the
       two oaths are?

170    Know that if you have sworn to take another's property
       or to take away from the holy church. For this I will not
       bring pardon, for know that neither an archbishop nor
       a bishop can do this; "The sin is not forgiven unless the
       theft is made good."

171    So help me God! The scriptures teach that if you have
       taken someone's goods wrongly, you should give them
       back; and if you have wrongly brought blame on any-
       one you cannot, so help me God, be quit of that blame
       until you have made things as they were before; you
       must take greater pain in restoring the good reputation
       than you took in establishing a bad one.

172    For, in God's name, thus says God, you must give back
       or hang at the gate and at the gibbet of hell.

173 Or ne dites mie, donques somes nous tout perdu; mais
vous devés dire, donques fait il malvais avoir de l'autrui
qui rendre ne le vuelt; et donques fait il mauvais faire à
autrui ce c'on ne feroit à lui meisme.

174 Après me sires li evesques si vous envoie pardon de tex
seremens comme on iure: La corone dieu! la teste dieu!
les plaies dieu! les angoisses dieu! le cuer dieu! le foie
dieu! les cleus dieu! le lance dieu! les hasquies dieu!
Tot depechie nostre segneur tout le desmenbres.

175 Car, si m'aït la mere dieu Sainte Marie! li bouchiers
ne depieche pas mex la char à son estal, que entre vous
depechiés nostre segneur entre vous pecheeur.

176 Si me consant la mere dieu Sainte Marie! I iors venra
que vous le comparrés quant nus hom ne nule fame ne
vous porra aidier, fors biens fais, ne grever, for pechiés.

177 Or oiés et etendés la plainte que nostre sires en fait à sa
bele compaignie de paradis: *Supra dorsum meum fabricaverunt peccatores.*

178 Mi ami, fait nostre segneur, cil pecheeur qui sunt en
terre forgent et fierent seur mon cors, par deseur mon
chief et par deseur tous mes menbres.

179 Entre vous, dame, iurés les: les menbres dieu! les ahins
dieu! le vertu dieu! le passion dieu! le pouche dieu! tout
depechie dieu et Sainte Marie.

180 Si m'aït Dieu! I'ai oï aucunes fois iurer tex seremens de
dieu et de Sainte Mere, que onques n'avint que seulement du rementevoir seroi ce grans pechiés.

173 Now do not say, "Then we are all lost!" Say instead, "Then it is bad to take others' goods and not want to return them, or to do others harm that one would not wish done to oneself."

174 Afterward my lord the bishop sends you pardon from such oaths, as one swears, "God's crown! God's head! God's wounds! God's agony! God's heart! God's liver! God's nails! God's lance! God's torments!" All these violate our Lord; all dismember him.

175 For, so help me Mother of God, Holy Mary, the butcher does not chop up the meat on his block more than you sinners tear the flesh of our Lord.

176 May the Mother of God give me her consent! The day will come when you will realize that no man or woman will be able to help you, but only your good works, or harm you, but only your sins.

177 Now listen and hear the complaint that our Lord made of this to his beautiful company in paradise: "The wicked have wrought upon my back."

178 My friends, says our Lord, the sinners who are on earth forge and strike my body, my head, and all my limbs.

179 Among yourselves, ladies, you swear thus: By God's limbs! By God's torments! By God's virtue! By God's passion! By God's mouth! All these violate God and Holy Mary.

180 God help me! I have sometimes heard such oaths sworn on God and on the Holy Mother that simply remembering them would be a great sin.

181   Biaus amis et tu bele amie, quant tu vas au marchié et
       tu as aucune chose à vendre ou à acater: Enon diu, fait-
       on donques, par les menbres, ne par la vie, ne par la
       cervele, ne par la boele, ge n'en donrai mie por mains,
       ou ge n'en donrai plus! Et plus en iurent, plus s'en
       pariurent li I et li autres ordement et desloiaument.

182   Après, beles douces gent, on a son seriant, on se
       courouche à lui par aucune aventure; or le met hors
       de son ostel; on iure quanque de dieu est, que iamais
       service ne li fera ne pour tant ne pour quant, ne pour
       cose que nus en die.

183   Après vient sire Hubers, sire Gautiers, dame Hersens,
       dame Aelis; si prient tant au preudome ou à la preude-
       fame qui ont fait les seremens, qu'il les font pariurer
       maugrés lor nés devant; or en aviegne du pechié le
       leu et le veel.

184   Après, bele douce gent, or se courouche à son voisin,
       ou par envie c'on a seur lui, ou par parole reporter,
       ou par tenchon, ou par merlée, ou par aucun acoison.

185   Enon Diu! cil qui ara le cuer felon et maulvais iura et
       teste, et cervele, et boele, et sanc et pis, et cuer, et plaies,
       [f. 137] et tout desmenbreront nostre segneur Ihesu
       Crist que iamais à lui ne parlera.

186   Lendemain ou au tiers ior on atorne, et venront prieur
       et prieresses qui tant iront entor, qu'il les feront parler
       ensanle et boire et mengier, et aler et parler ensanle.

181 Good friend, and you, my good lady friend, when you go to the market to buy or sell something, "By the name of God," you might say, "by God's limbs" or " life" or "brain" or "entrails," "I shall not give it for a penny less; or I shall not pay more for it!" And the more they swear, the more they duly and treacherously perjure themselves.

182 Then, good gentlefolk, you have a servant, you get angry with him for some reason; you throw him out of his lodging; you swear by whatever part of God's body that you will never in any way help him—no matter what happens or what anyone says.

183 And then, along come Lord Hubert, Lord Gautier, Lady Hersens, Lady Alice; they so beseech the good man or good woman who had sworn to falsely swear away the nose on their face; this is what comes of the sin of the wolf and the calf.

184 And then, good gentlefolk, they get angry at their neighbor, either through jealousy or hearsay, or over a quarrel or a fight or for some other reason.

185 By the name of God! The evil-hearted will swear by the head, brain, entrails, blood and chest [*also* piss], heart and wounds of our Lord, and all [that] will rend our Lord Jesus Christ apart, that they shall never speak to [that neighbor] again.

186 The next day or the day after they make peace with each other. And then come the priors and prioresses, who go about so much that they get them to talk and drink and eat together, and walk and talk together.

187    Et plus et tot ce pris ge bien à avoir amor et compaignie
les uns avec les autres, mais que li diables ne seme
aucune mauvaise semence ou de luxure ou de glouter
ou de trop boire ou de trop mengier; mais ie blasme
et repreng les grans seremens et les haus c'on a pariuré
de nostre segneur. Ausi fait dex meismes.

188    Biaus amis et tu bele amie, ia certes ne iuerras le corone
de nostre segneur que tu ne li renoveles les grans doleurs
qu'il eut à son cuer; car saches tu bien, ele fu moult tren-
chans et moult poignans la sainte corone, qu'ele fu de
rosel marin trenchant et d'aubes espines poignans.

189    Et sachiés c'on li enforma en son chief si souef, c'on li
percha son beneoit cuir et sa beneoite char desi qu'à son
benoit tes et desi c'à ses glorieus os, que nostre segneur
fu arousés de son benoit sanc et devant et derriere.

190    Ià certes ne iuerrés la benoite teste dieu que vous ne li
renovelés les angoisses qu'il soufri à la corone enformer
en son glorieus chief. Ià certes de cele eure ne iuerrés les
plaies nostre segneur que vous ne li ramentevés les grans
angoisses qu'il eut à son cuer, quant Longis li percha son
beneoit cuer.

191    Ià certes riens ne iuerrés de nostre segneur que vous
tous ses tormens ne li renovelés.

192    Quant vos iurés ses espaules, vous faites de vostre langue
martel, si l'en ferés seur ses beles espaules.

193    Quant vous iurés les paumes, les piés, tos les biaus
menbres nostre segneur totes les fois que vous les iurés,
vous le ferés seur ses glorieus menbres.

187    And indeed I reckon it is good that they should love
       one another and seek each other's company, but may
       the devil sow no bad seed; whether of lust or gluttony
       or drinking or eating too much. But I condemn and
       reprove the great and lofty oaths with which you
       have perjured our Lord. And God does the same.

188    Good friend, and you, my good lady friend, indeed,
       do not swear by the crown of our Lord lest you rekindle
       the great sufferings in his heart; for know well that the
       holy crown was very sharp and cutting, being made of
       sharp water reeds and of dagger-like hawthorn.

189    And know that they thrust it on his sweet head, pierc-
       ing his blessed skin and his blessed flesh through to his
       blessed head and his glorious bones, so that our Lord
       was bathed in his blessed blood both in front and
       behind.

190    Indeed, you must certainly not swear upon the blessed
       head of God, or you will renew the agonies that he suf-
       fered from the crown thrust on his glorious head. Do
       not ever swear by God's wounds, or you will remind
       him of the great anguish that he had in his heart when
       Longinus pierced his blessed heart.

191    Indeed, do not swear on any part of our Lord, lest you
       renew his torments.

192    When you swear by God's shoulders, you turn your
       tongue into a hammer to beat his beautiful shoulders.

193    When you swear on the hands, the feet, all the beautiful
       limbs of our Lord, every time that you swear on them,
       you wound his glorious limbs.

194 Toutes les fois que vous iurés le sanc dieu et les cleus
nostre segneur vous li renovelés les grans angoisses qu'il
souffri au fichier en la crois; que l'escriture raconte que
onques [pressoir *deleted*] raisins en pressoir ne fu si à
destroit comme fu la beneoite chars nostre segneur
entre le fer et le fust.

195 Ià certes ne iuerrés les estaches là u li cors nostre segneur
fu loiés, que vous ne li renovelés le batement qu'il i
souffri, dont on li ronpi et trencha de grans corgies
nouées se benoite char desi c'à ses beneois os.

196 Ia certes la dame ne iuerra de cele eure la bouche Dieu
c'on ne li renovele le bouire dont il fu abuvrés de fiel et
d'aisil en l'autel de la sainte vraie crois.

197 Ia certes la dame ne iuerra de cele eure le passion dieu
qu'ele ne li renovele les grans hontes et les grans laidures
et les grans vilenies qu'il soffri; car li dous dieu il i souffri
qu'il i fu ferus et batus et boutés et bufiés et laidengiés et
crucefiés et escopis en mi son beneoit visage.

198 Et sachiés bele douce gent, par bone verité que ie vous
monstre orendroit en ceste pieche de terre, que entre
vous qui creés en nostre segneur et qui bien savés qu'il
vous fist de si povre chose comme du limon de la terre
faites graigneur pechié de tant seulement que vous iurés
si fais seremens de nostre segneur que ne firent li Iuis
qui le crucefierent, ne sil qui le loierent à l'estache,
ne cil qui le batirent.

199 Certes veés ent le tesmongnage del escriture: *Oportebat
pati Cristum et resurgere a mortuis, et ita intrare in gloriam
suam.*

194    Every time that you swear by God's blood or by our
       Lord's nails, you renew the great passion that he suf-
       fered stretched on the cross; the scriptures relate that
       never was a grape in the winepress so tightly squeezed
       as was the blessed flesh of our Lord between iron and
       wood.

195    Indeed, now, do not swear by the whipping post to
       which the body of our Lord was bound, lest you renew
       the beating he suffered when he was broken and
       scourged with great knotted cords that furrowed
       his blessed flesh to the bones.

196    Indeed, a lady who then swears by God's mouth only
       renews the gall and vinegar that he was given to drink
       on the altar of the True Cross.

197    Indeed, a lady should not then swear on the Passion
       of God, lest she renew for him the great shame and
       the great ugliness and the great villainy he suffered; for
       sweet God endured being struck, beaten, hit, buffeted,
       vilified, crucified, and spat upon in his blessed face.

198    Good gentlefolk, I shall now show you truly on this bit
       of earth that those of you who believe in our Lord and
       know that he has made you of humble clay sin more
       when you swear by our Lord than the Jews who cruci-
       fied him, or the ones who bound him to the stake and
       beat him.

199    Indeed, see what the scriptures say: "Ought not Christ
       to have suffered and rise from the dead and enter into
       his glory."

200   Certes il ne savoient qu'il il estoit li vrais sires, ains cui-
      doient sans doute que ce fust uns lerres, I traitres, I faus
      profetes; que saciés vraiement que se il seussent certaine-
      ment qu'il fust li vrais dieu, ançois si fussent il laissié
      pendre et trainer et ardoir et escorchier et lapider ce
      sachiés vraiement, qu'il l'eussent [f. 137v] traitié à tel
      honte?

201   Et sans faille l'escriture tesmoigne que il covenoit nostre
      segneur souffrir ces tormens c'on li faisoit, et qu'il resu-
      sitast de mort à vie, et qu'il montast là sus en sa gloire.

202   Certes il covenoit par fine force que li tirant feissent
      ces laidures à nostre segneur; car autrement eust nostre
      segneur fait tort à tous les diables d'enfer de lor ames
      qu'il avoient gaaigniés; pour seulement du commande-
      ment que nostre segneur avoit fait à Adam nostre pri-
      merain pere at à Eve nostre primeraine mere, que pour
      seulement le pome que il mengierent par l'enortement
      du diable.

203   Car sachiés, Eve fu primes dechuté, et quant ele vit
      qu'ele fu engingnié, ainc ne fist autre chose, mais vint
      à Adan son baron, si l'engingne et si le dechut; onques
      ne fu à aise, onques ne fu lie, quant ele se trova si nue,
      si despollié, ains eut ausi Adan despoillié.

204   Car saciés, par l'oncion que ge aportai des sains fons
      là u ge fui bautisiés et levés! car il estoient vestu de le
      gloire nostre segneur, ne ne se pooient veir; puis le chaut
      en avalent, et tantost il seurent bien apertement qu'il
      avoient mal ovré, et tantost se virent apertement li I
      l'autre.

200      Indeed, they did not know he was the true Lord, and so they thought no doubt that he was a thief, a traitor, a false prophet. For surely had they known that he was the true God, they would not have let him be hanged and dragged and burned and flayed and stoned. Would they really have treated him so shamefully?

201      Holy scripture certainly shows that it was right and proper for our Lord to suffer the torments inflicted on him and to rise from the dead to life and to ascend to heaven in glory.

202      It was indeed essential that the tyrants should so maltreat our Lord, for it was thus that our Lord deprived all the devils in hell of the souls that they had won, on account only of our Lord's command to Adam and Eve, our first father and mother, and only because of the apple that they ate at the devil's behest.

203      For know that Eve was first to fall, and when she saw that she was deceived, what else did she do but to go to Adam, her lord, to deceive him and bring him down? Never again was she happy or at ease, finding herself so naked and despoiled, and having despoiled Adam as well.

204      For be sure by the unction that I bring from the holy font where I was baptized and washed, that they were dressed in the glory of our Lord and could not see their nakedness; then they fell from [glory] and knew at once that they had done evil, and at once they saw each other openly.

205  Et adonc eut tel honte li I de l'autre qu'il prisent cascuns
une fueille de figuier, se le mirent devant leur menbées
et devant lor humanités, dont ge n'os ore pas faire men-
sion, si se muchierent, et nostre segneur dieu veoit tout
cest afaire, et que fist li vrais dieu au deerain? *Post
meridiem, clamavit et dixit: Adam, ubi es?*

206  Bele douce gent, à l'eure après midi si vint nostre segneur si apela Adam et si li dist: *Adam, ubi es?* Et que
respondit Adans *Audivi, Domine, vocem tuam et
absondi* [sic] *me.*

207  Sire, sire, ge ai oïe ta vois, fist Adans, et ge me sui
muchiés, et repus, car ge me trovai tous nus.

208  Sire, Eve m'a traï.

209  *Ecce Adam quasi ex vobis* [*recte* nobis] *unus factus est,
sciens bonum et malum; videte ne forte sumat de ligno vite.*

210  Adam, Adam, dist nostre segneur, e ne t'avoie ge fait et
formé à ma forme, et tout otroié et abandoné, paradis
et terre et mer et poissons et bestes sauvages et oisiaus
volans, et t'avoie doné sens et raison et entendement
et de savoir et de de bien et de mal; et se t'avoie def-
fendu que tu ne mengasses pas del fruit de mon arbre.

211  Pour coi es tu plus tost asentis as commandemens du
diable que à mes commandemens?

212  Sachiés bien que tu le comperas, car tu seras en paine
et en dolour et en ahans toute ta vie et quanque de toi
istera, et après ta mort tu t'en iras hors de paradis.

213  *Cherubin et flammeum gladium atque versatilem.*

205　And each was so ashamed before the other that they took a fig leaf and put it in front of their member and in front of their humanity—of which I do not dare to make mention—thus they covered themselves, and our Lord God saw the entire affair. What did the true God do then? "After the noon hour he called and said, 'Adam, where are you?'"

206　Good sweet people, at the hour after noon our Lord came and called Adam and said to him, "Adam, where are you?" And what did Adam answer? "I heard, Lord, your voice, and I hid.

207　"Lord, Lord, I heard your voice," said Adam, "and I went and hid, for I found myself entirely naked.

208　"Lord, Eve betrayed me."

209　Behold, Adam is become one of us, knowing good and evil; see that he not grasp the tree of life again.

210　"Adam, Adam," said our Lord, "did I not make you and form you in my form and bestow on you all things— paradise and earth, sea and fish, wild beasts and birds of the air—and did I not give you sense and reason and understanding both of good and of evil, and did I not forbid you to eat of the fruit of my tree?

211　"Why have you sooner obeyed the devil's commandments than mine?

212　"Know that you will pay for this, for you will be in pain and suffering and in labor all your life, and [so will] those who come after you, and after your death you will go away from paradise."

213　"[And he placed] cherubim with a flaming double-edged sword."

214    Adonc vint li angles nostre segneur si bouta Evam et
Adam hor de paradis, et vesquirent en dolor et en paine
toute lor vie, si comme nous faisons encore cascun iour,
et saciés que se ne fust li trespas del commandement que
Eve et Adams firent, iamais ne nous esteust ne maïn
lever ne tart couchier, ne estre en paine de boire ne
de mengier ne de vestir, ne de cauchier; tout fu siens
saoulé de veir les grans gloires de paradis.

215    Beles douce gent, saciés que dès le tans Aden dusc' à
l'eure que li dous rois de paradis prist incarnation en
la douce virge Sainte Marie, ne nasquit hom ne fame
de ventre de mere que tout n'alassent es en la mort et
es tormens d'enfer dont dex nous gart tous et totes par
sa grant pitié et par sa grant misericorde.

216    Bele douce gent, quant nostre segneur vit que tout estoit
perdu par I home quanque il avoit fait comme de son
*[missing word]* le si resgarda que tout ausi comme il estoient perdu par I home qui onques ne fu engenrés, si
covenoit il ausi qu'il fust sauvés par I home qui onques
ne fu engenrés.

217    Et pour ce manda nostre segneur à la [f. 138] Sainte
Verge le salus qu'il s'aumberoit en li, et dont li dist li
angles, *Ave Maria gratia plena, Dominus tecum.*

218    Et pour ce vous di ge ore: il covenoit par fine force que
nostre segneur descendist des chieus et qu'il s'aumbrast
en Sainte Marie et qu'il soffrist les tormens en le sainte
Crois pour son pule rachater, qui estoit en enfer, et il
ne veut nulus faire tort; car autrement eust il fait tort
as diables d'enfer.

214    And then came the angel of our Lord who drove Eve and Adam away from paradise, and they lived in misery and pain all their lives, just as we do now every day, and know that had Eve and Adam not broken the commandment, we would never have to get up early or go to bed late, we would never need to drink or eat or dress ourselves or put on shoes; they had everything, and were overjoyed to see the great glory of paradise.

215    Good gentlefolk, know that from the time of Adam to the hour that the sweet King of paradise was made flesh in the sweet Virgin, Holy Mary, there was no man or woman born of a mother's womb who did not die and go to the torments of hell, from which God save us all, men and women, in his great pity and great mercy.

216    Good gentlefolk, when our Lord saw that all was lost by the fault of a man, whom he had made *[missing word],* he saw that just as everything had been lost by a man who was not conceived, it was fitting that everything be saved by a man not conceived.

217    And therefore our Lord sent the Holy Virgin the salvation by which he caused her to be with child and of which the angel said, "Hail Mary, full of grace, the Lord is with thee."

218    And therefore I say unto you, it was essential that our Lord descend from heaven and become flesh in Saint Mary and suffer on the Holy Cross to redeem his people, who were in hell, and he wanted to do wrong to no one, for otherwise he would have deprived the devils in hell [of the souls they had won].

219 Il covenoit par vive force que li tirant li fecissent et
desissent toutes les hontes, toutes les felenies que il li
dirent et firent; mais certes cest dieu, il ne vous covent
mie que vous iurés les vilains seremens de nostre segneur, pour ce, dist l'escriture, que entre vous faites plus
grans pechiés qui ainsi iurés de dieu et de sa mere, et de
saints et de saintes tout le depechiés, tout le dehechiés
plus que ne firent li tirant, li traitres qui le crucefierent.

220 De tous ces pechiés mesire li evesques vous envoie pardon et asolucion à tous ciaus et à toutes celes qui leur
aumosnes envoieront à l'eglise me dame Sainte Marie
d'Amiens; ausi cuite s'en iront hui à ceste sainte matinée, comme fist la sainte Madeleine des biaus piés
nostre segneur. Or prions dieu et sa douce mere que
disnement le vous laist rechevoir.

221 Après, bele douce gent, mesire li evesques vous envoie
pardon et asolucion de totes les foles fiances que vous
onques feistes, mais que ce ne fust pour autrui catel tolir
ou por autrui desireter, car saciés on acroit une dete seur
sa fiance, on afie sa fiance li I à l'autre en sa iovence, par
enfance ou par envoiseure ou par sotie, se li varlés puet
enginnier la meschine; ia puis sa fiance ne regardera et
qui a fait la folie, si le gart.

222 En non Dieu, vous n'en estes pas cuites de la fiance.

223 Ore, bele douce gent, on doit une dete sur sa fiance;
on ne le puet paier ou par maladie ou par oubliance ou
par essoigne de cors; quant on vient au deteur, il prent
volentiers la dete et bien vous quite de la dete; mais
il ne vous cuite mie la fiance, car il n'i a pooir.

219 It was entirely appropriate that the tyrants said and did all sorts of shameful and cruel thing to him, but so help me God, it is not appropriate for you to swear the loathsome oaths by our Lord, for the scriptures teach that you sin more grievously by so swearing on God and his mother and on the saints and thereby harm him more than the tyrants and traitors who crucified him.

220 My lord the bishop sends pardon and absolution from all these sins to all men and women who send their alms to the church of my Lady, Saint Mary of Amiens; and so they will leave today on this holy morning as free [of sin] as Saint Mary Magdalene when she went from the beautiful feet of our Lord. Now let us pray God and his sweet mother that you will worthily receive [this pardon].

221 Then, good gentlefolk, my lord the bishop sends you pardon and absolution for all the foolish undertakings into which you have entered, except for seizing another's property or disinheriting someone, for know that you take on a debt upon a promise, and you may pledge your word, whether through childish inexperience, through whim, or through stupidity. If the manservant can inveigle the maid and does not keep his promise . . . well, then, let he who has committed the folly watch out.

222 In God's name, you are not quit of the promise.

223 Now, good gentlefolk, you may owe a debt upon a pledge and cannot pay it because of sickness or forgetfulness or because you are physically unable; when you come to the creditor he may readily assume the debt and release you from it, but he cannot free you from the promise to repay, because he does not have the power.

224 Mesire li evesques i a pooir en teles fiances pardoner,
mais que les detes soient [pardonés *deleted*] rendues c'on
a acreues seur les fiances, aquité vous en irés hui en cest
ior du pechié et de la peneance, comme fist Saint Pierre
du renoiement qu'il fist de nostre segneur qui III fois
l'avait renoié.

225 Proiés à nostre segneur que vrai pardon vous en face
à tous chiaus et à toutes celes qui leur aumosnes et leur
biaus dons envoieront à l'eglise Nostre Dame Sainte
Marie d'Amiens.

226 Après, bele douce gent, mesire li evesques vous envoie
pardon et asolucion de totes les coses terrienes que vous
avés eu de l'autrui par male desraison; de tant com vous
en envoierés à l'eglise ma dame Sainte Marie d'Amiens,
de tant serés quite, soit de tout, soit de le moitié, soit du
quartier.

227 Et d'autre partie I chevaliers ou I autres hom va en ost
ou en torner ou en chevauchié ou en pelerinage, aucune
fois ont eu de tes coses ou de trueve ou d'aucune aventure, si m'aït dieu nostre segneur vous n'i avés droit
du retenir que vous ne l'avés pas gaaignié: ou rendre
ou pendre, ce dist dieu en l'escriture, que par les sains
de chaiens ne par le sacrement que on fait de nostre
segneur.

228 Ge estoie à une Pentecoste à Abevile en Pontieu desus
l'autel d'une eglise c'on apele Saint Sepuchre; or m'en
sovient par cest mot: *veritas non querit angulos,* vérités
ne loiautés n'a cure d'angles; *Deus est veritas,* dex est
verités; ce dist l'escriture.

224    My lord the bishop is empowered to pardon such
       pledges. So long as the debts that have been accrued
       on the promises are repaid, you shall be acquitted today
       of sin and of penance, as was Saint Peter for denying
       our Lord three times.

225    Pray to our Lord to grant true pardon to all those men
       and women who send their alms and their fine gifts to
       the church of Notre-Dame, Saint Mary of Amiens.

226    Then, good gentlefolk, my lord the bishop sends you
       pardon and absolution for all the legal suits that have
       been wrongly brought against you. For the amount
       that you send to the church of my Lady, Saint Mary
       of Amiens, you shall be quit accordingly of the whole
       sum, the half, or the quarter.

227    Likewise, a knight or another man goes to war or a
       tournament or on a military campaign or a pilgrimage
       and at some time has acquired such things either by
       finding them or by some other circumstance, so help
       me God! You have no right to keep what is not yours:
       give it back or hang, says our Lord in the scriptures, as
       well as by the local saints and by the Lord's sacrament.

228    One Pentecost I was at Abbeville, in Ponthieu, in front
       of the altar of a church dedicated to the Holy Sepulcher;
       now I remember [it] by this saying, *veritas non quaerit
       angulos:* truth and honesty do not search for angles.
       *Deus est veritas,* God is truth; so says scripture.

229 Ilueques fui à la parole nostre segneur d'un bon maistre
frère Wedoir de Danrichier; iacobins est et preudon
et bons clers, et saciés qu'il a poesté de preechier la foi
nostre segneur par tote [f. 138v] l'evesquié d'Amiens
et est peneanchiers mon segneur l'evesque.

230 Iluec conta d'un marcheant qui venoit d'une feste la
u il avoit mené grant marcheandise et moult vendi.

231 Bientot tout son avoir mist en une masse d'or molu; erra
par ses iournées et tant qu'il passa parmi une bone vile,
comme est Amiens ou Paris ou une autre bone ville; et
passa par devant une eglise.

232 Li preudon qui avoit à usage de faire ses oroisons devant
l'image de la mere deu Sainte Marie, ala au mostier et
fist ses ouroisons et mist son gourle delès lui.

233 Quant il se leva d'ourer, avaine pensée qu'il eut li fist
oublier son avoir, et s'en ala, ne ne s'en dona garde.

234 I borgois avoit en la vile, qui ausinc avoit acoustumé
d'aler au mostier, et moult volentiers et sovent faisoit
ses oroisons devant la beneoite mere de nostre segneur
Sainte Marie.

235 Iluec trova ce grant avoir, et vit qu'il estoit seelées et
bien fermés à I loquet; si estut et si s'esmerveilla dont
cil avoirs venoit; Hée dex! dist-il, que ferai ge? Se ge
le fas savoir aval cele vile que ge aie trové cest avoir, tex
le clamera qui onques n'i ot paine ne travail à l'aquerre.

236 Adonc se porpensa li borgois qu'il le garderoit dusa [il
*deleted*] icele eure qu'il en aroit vraies noveles.

229　There I heard the sermon of our Lord given by a good
　　master, Friar Wedoir of Saint-Riquier, a Dominican
　　and an honest man and good cleric, and know that
　　he has the authority to preach the faith of our Lord
　　throughout the diocese of Amiens and is the confessor
　　of my lord the bishop.

230　There he told of a merchant who was coming from a
　　fair to which he had brought much merchandise and
　　where he had sold a great deal.

231　With all his wealth soon put in a lump of milled gold,
　　he traveled for days until he came to a large city, like
　　Amiens or Paris or another large city, and he passed
　　in front of a church.

232　The good man who was accustomed to saying his
　　prayers before the image of the Mother of God, Saint
　　Mary, went to the church and said his prayers, putting
　　his purse close by him.

233　When he got up from praying, he carelessly forgot his
　　property and left, not paying attention.

234　There was a townsman who was also accustomed to
　　going to church; gladly and often he would pray before
　　the [statue of the] blessed mother of our Lord, Saint
　　Mary.

235　There he found this great treasure and saw that it was
　　sealed and fully closed with a clasp, and he was surprised
　　and wondered where it had come from. "God!" he said,
　　"What shall I do? If I report in town what I have found,
　　someone who did not work for it will claim it."

236　So he decided to keep it until he had some real informa-
　　tion about it.

237   Vint en sa cambre et mist cel avoir dedans I escrin,
et vint à son wis et escrit d'une marle grosse une grosse
letre, *Quicunques aroit riens perdu qu'il venist à lui.*

238   Quant li marcheans eut erré grant piece et il fu hors
de sa pensée, tasta entour lui et quida trover son gourle;
n'en trouva mie.

239   Adonc fu moult à mesaise. Alas! dist-il, tout ai perdu!
mors sui! traïs sui!

240   Il s'en revint au mostier et cuida trover son gourle,
n'en trova mie.

241   Il vint au prestre, demanda noveles de son avoir, n'en
trova nule.

242   Issi du mostier tout pensant, trova ces letres escrites
en l'uis; si entra en l'ostel, et vit le borgois, qui l'avoit
trové et dist, Ha! sire, par diu, estes vous sires de cest
ostel? Oïl, dist il, sire, tant comme dieu plaira; que plaist
vous?

243   Ha! sire, dist li marcheans, par dieu, dites moi qui escrit
ces letres en votre huis? Et li bourgois se faint ansi
comme s'il n'en seust riens.

244   Biaus amis, dit li borgois, il repaire chaiens gens et
clercs; si escrisent lors vers, lors deduis.

245   Biaus sire, et que voliés vous? Avés vous riens perdu?
Perdu! sire, dist li marcheans; certes ge ai perdu si grant
avoir que ge ne le sai nonbrer. Coment, biaus amis, dist
li borgois, c'as-tu perdu? Certes, sire, i'ai perdu I gorle
tout plain *[illegible deletion]* d'or seelé à tel seel et à tel
loquet!

237 Having entered his room and put the treasure in a chest, he wrote in big letters on his door with a big piece of chalk, "Anybody who has lost anything, apply here."

238 The merchant, distracted, having walked a long way, searched about himself for his purse but could not find it.

239 And then he was extremely upset. "Alas," he said, "I have lost everything; I might as well be dead! I am betrayed!"

240 He went back to the church and tried to find his purse but could not.

241 He went to the priest and asked if he had information about his money, but there was none.

242 Leaving the church, deep in thought, he found the writing on the door; he went into the house and saw the townsman who had found the money. "Ha! Lord, by God!" he said, "Are you the master of this lodging?" "Yes, Lord," said the other, "thanks be to God. What can I do for you?"

243 "Ha! Lord," said the merchant, "for God's sake, tell me who wrote the words on your door?" And the townsman pretended he knew nothing about it.

244 "Good friend," said the townsman, "both laymen and clerics come here; they write their rhymes and whatever comes into their heads.

245 "Good sir, what do you want? Have you lost anything?" "Lost anything! Sir," said the merchant, "I have indeed lost more money than I can count." "How so, good friend?" said the townsman, "What have you lost?" "Indeed, Sir, I have lost a purse full of gold, sealed with such and such a seal and such and such a clasp."

246 Adonc seut li borgois qu'il avoit dite verités; adonc
l'apela le marcheant en sa cambre et li mostra
le grant avoir, et si li rova prendre.

247 Et quant li marcheans trova le borgois de loiauté si
plains, si estut, et pensa; Biaus sire dieu, dist li marcheans, ge ne sui pas disnes d'avoir tel avoir et tel tresor
comme ge avoie amassé. Cist borgois en est plus disnes
que ge ne sui.

248 Sire, dist li marcheans, certes li avoir est bien enploiés
en vous mex qu'en moi, et ge le vous doins, et à dieu
vous commant.

249 Ha! biaus amis, dist li borgois, p[r]en ton avoir, ge ne
l'ai pas deservi.

250 Certes ne ferai, dist li marcheans, gel ne'l prendrai pas,
ains m'en irai m'arme sauver. Si s'en fui grant aleure.

251 Et quant li borgois vit qu'il s'en aloit si durement si va
après lui et commence à crier: Larron! larron! Pernés
le larron! Et quant si voisin virent celui qui s'enfuioit,
si vont, si le prendent et dient au borgois: Que vous a
cist hom meffait et enblé?

252 Certes, segneur, dist li borgois, il me velt embler ma
verité et ma loiauté, que ge ai gardée desicà ore. Si lor
conta la verité et quant li borgois *[illegible deletion]* de
son visnage oïrent la verité, si font prendre au marcheant son avoir tout //

246  Then the townsman knew that the merchant had told the truth, and he invited him to his room and showed him the great treasure and asked him to take it.

247  And finding the townsman so honest, so intelligent, the merchant thought, "Good Lord God," said the merchant, "I do not deserve to have the great fortune and treasure I have amassed. This townsman deserves it more than I."

248  "Sir," said the merchant, "indeed, you can make better use of the treasure than I, and I give it to you, and commend you to God."

249  "Ha! good friend," said the townsman, "take your treasure; I do not deserve it."

250  "Indeed, I shall not," said the merchant. "By not taking it, I shall save my soul." So he ran off at great speed.

251  And when the townsman saw the merchant running away so hard he ran after him shouting, "Thief! thief! Stop, thief!" And when the neighbors saw the man who was fleeing, they chased him and caught him and said to the townsman, "What harm has this man done you, and what has he stolen?"

252  "Indeed, Sirs," said the townsman, "he wants to steal my truth and my honesty that I have kept up until now." So he told them the truth; and when the neighbors heard the truth, they made the merchant take all his treasure. //

APPENDIX

# SOURCES QUOTED IN THE SERMON

The version found in the sermon is given first, followed by the author and, for biblical quotations, the Vulgate text (with the speaker name in parentheses). I wish to acknowledge the help I received from Consuelo Dutschke in locating sources.

6     *Maior est obedientia quam victima; . . . [maior est obedientia] quem victime.* / 1 Samuel 15:22, *Melior est enim oboedientia quam victimae* (Samuel).

10    *Ubi te invenero, ibi te iudicabo.* / Found in Abbot Suger's *Vita Ludovici Grossi (Patrologiae cursus completus, series latina,* ed. J.-P. Migne [Paris, 1841–64; hereafter *PL*], 186.1326b) but not in the scriptures: "Haec verba in sacris Scripturis non occurrent" (ibid., n. 363).

13    *consummatum est.* / John 19:30, *consummatum est* (Christ).

14    *Probatio dilectonis exibitio est operit, dixit beatus Gregorius.* / Gregory the Great, Homiliarum XL in Evangelia, book 2, homily 30, chapter 1, line 19, *Dilectionis exhibitio est operis.*

20     *Increpasti superbos maledicti qui declinant a mandatis tuis.* /
       Psalm 118:21, *Increpasti superbos maledicti qui recedunt a*
       *mandatis tuis* (David).

22     *Dilige proximum tuum sicut te ipsum* / Matthew 19:19, *diliges*
       *proximum tuum sicut te ipsum* (Christ). See also Matthew
       22:39, Mark 12:31 and 33, Luke 10:27, Romans 13:9,
       Galatians 5:14, and James 2:8.

39     *Non incipienti sed perseveranti dabitur corona.* / Matthew 10:
       22, *Qui autem perseveraverit in finem hic salvus erit* (Christ).
       The idea exists in multiple forms.

47     *ad quod venisti?* / Matthew 26:50, *Amice, ad quod venisti?*
       (Christ to Judas).

57     *Qui facit elemosinam, nesciat sinistra tua quid faciat dextera*
       *tua.* / Matthew 6:3, *te autem faciente elemosynam nesciat*
       *sinistra tua quid faciat dextera tua* (Christ).

61     *Dimissa sunt ei peccata quoniam dilexit multum.* / Luke 7:47,
       *Remittentur ei peccata multa quoniam dilexit multum* (Christ).

63     *Apostola apostolorum.* / This phrase obviously does not occur
       in the Gospels. The idea may come from Matthew 28:7–8,
       where Mary Magdalene is sent by the angels to announce
       Christ's resurrection to the Apostles.

65     *Qui honorem honorem, et qui tributum tributum.* / Romans
       13:7, *Reddite omnibus debita, cui tributum tributum . . . cui*
       *honorem honorem* (Paul).

77     *quia quem celi capere non poterant, tuo gremio contulisti.* /
       Liturgical, the third response for the second nocturn at ma-
       tins on Christmas Day, *quia quem coeli capere non poterant*
       *tuo gremio contulisti.*

80     *Velle eius, velle dei; nolle eius, nolle sui.* / Devotional, the
       prayer adressed to the Virgin and John the Evangelist,
       *O Intemerata et in eternum benedicta . . . Credo enim firmiter*
       *et fateor indubitanter quia velle vestrum, velle Dei est; et nolle*
       *vestrum nolle Dei est.*

83     *Salve sancta parens, enixa puerpera regem.* / Liturgical, the
introit for a mass of the Virgin between the feast of the
Purification (2 Feb.) and Advent (c. 30 Nov.), *Salve sancta
parens, enixa puerpera regem. . . .*

98     *quo loco, quo tempore.* / Acts 1:7, *non est vestrum nosse tempora
vel momenta.* Possibly also of judicial origin.

121     *Respondens, Simon Petrus dixit* / Matthew 16:16, *respondens
Simon Petrus dixit.* Also Luke 9:20.

122     *Beatus es, Simon Bariona quia caro et sanguis non revelavit tibi
sed pater meus qui est in celis; et ego dico tibi quia tu es Petrus et
super hanc petram edificabo ecclesiam meam et porte inferi non
prevalebunt adversus eum, et tibi dabo claves regni celorum et
quoque solveris super terram erit solutum et in celis, et quoque
ligaveris super terram erit ligatum in celis.* / Matthew 16:17–
19, *Beatus es Simon Bar Iona quia caro et sanguis non revelavit
tibi sed Pater meus qui in caelis est. Et ego dico tibi quia tu es
Petrus et super hanc petram aedificabo ecclesiam meam et portae
inferi non praevalebunt adversum eam et tibi dabo claves regni
caelorum et quodcumque ligaveris super terram erit ligatum et
in caelis et quodcumque solveris super terram erit solutum in
caelis* (Christ).

137     *Sola dies purgatorium super omnes sanctorum omnium* (Augustine). The precise source is unknown.

141     "Dont Saint Gregoire nous tesmoigne en cel maniere: Escri-
siés, fait Saint Gregoire, 1 fu de vermeilles couleurs. . . ." /
Possibly from Gregory's *Homiliae in Exechielem,* especially
homilies 7 and 9, which draw on Psalm 117:12.

152     *Miseremini, miseremini mei, saltem vos amici mei, quia manus
Domini tetigit me.* / Job 19:21, *Miseremini mei, miseremini
mei saltim vos amici mei quia manus Domini tetigit me* (Job).

160     *Dignus est operarius mercede sua.* Luke 10:7, *dignus enim est
operarius mercede sua* (Christ). Also 1 Timothy 5:18.

170     *Non dimittitur peccatum, nisi restituatur ablatum.* / Augustine,
    *Epistula* 153 (in *Diversis quaestionibus ad Simplicianum,* ed.
    Almut Mutzenbecher, *Corpus Christianorum, series latina,*
    vol. 44 [Turnhout, 1970], pars 6, p. 419, line 5).

177     *Supra dorsum meum fabricaverunt peccatores.* / Psalm 128:3,
    *Super cervicem meam arabant arantes prolongaverunt sulcum
    suum.*

199     *Oportebat pati Cristum et resurgere a mortuis, et ita intrare
    in gloriam suam.* / Acts 17:3, *quia Christum oportuit pati
    et resurgere a mortuis.* Luke 24:26, *Nonne haec oportuit pati
    Christum et ita intrare in gloriam suam?* See also John 20:9.

205     *Post meridiem, clamavit et dixit: Adam, ubi es?* / Genesis 3:
    9–10, *Vocavitque Dominus Deus Adam et dixit ei: Ubi es. Qui
    ait: Vocem tuam audivi in paradiso et timui eo quod nudus essem
    et abscondi me.*

206     *Adam, ubi es? Audivi, Domine, vocem tuam et absondi me.* /
    See under 205.

209     *Ecce Adam quasi ex vobis unus factus est, sciens bonum et malum;
    videte ne forte sumat de ligno vite.* / Genesis 3:22, *Ecce Adam
    nobis factus est quasi unus ex sciens bonum et malum; nunc ergo,
    ne forte mittat manum suam et sumat etiam de ligno vitae....*

213     *Cherubin et flammeum gladium atque versatilem.* / Genesis
    3:24, *cherubin et flammeum gladium atque versatilem.*

217     *Ave Maria gratia plena, Dominus tecum.* / Luke 1:28, *Have
    gratia plena Dominus tecum benedicta tu in mulieribus* (the
    angel Gabriel). A very common prayer of devotional and
    liturgical origin.

228     *veritas non querit angulos* / Hans Walther, ed., *Proverbia
    sententiaeque latinitatis Medii Aevi,* Carmina Medii Aevi
    posterioris latina, vol. 5 (Göttingen, 1967), 673.
    *Deus est veritas* / John 14:6, *Dicit ei Iesus: Ego sum via
    et veritas et vita.*

# NOTES

## INTRODUCTION

1. The catalogue entry is derived from Dom Grenier's notation attached to his transcription of the sermon in volume 14 of the collection, fol. 64: "Sermon picard du 13ᵉ siècle fait, je crois, à l'occasion de la construction de la cathédrale d'Amiens." For the catalogue of the collection, see Philippe Lauer, *Collections manuscrits sur l'histoire des provinces de France: Inventaire,* vol. 2: *Périgord-Vexin* (Paris, 1911). The collection is described as "notes et documents relatifs à la liturgie, l'histoire, les superstitions, jeux, mystères, mœurs et usages de Picardie."

The original manuscript (vol. 158, fols. 131–38) consists of eight parchment leaves measuring about 16.5 × 21 cm. The parchment is of mediocre quality, and on page 7 the scribe has written his text around a hole. The leaves were once bound together in a little book probably made up of four or five bifolios; traces remain of the original gutter and stitch marks between bifolios. The last page, which was perhaps an attached folio, is lost. The text is written in two columns, with thirty four lines to the page; prick marks and line markings are still visible. The script, which seems to be from about the middle of the thirteenth century (slightly earlier according to Consuelo Dutschke, slightly later according to Harvey Stahl and Alison Stones, to whom I owe thanks), is in black ink with red ink decoration applied to certain initials. The first page is embellished with a decorative initial *B*. There is no title at the top of the page; at the bottom, an eighteenth-century hand has inscribed the words "Collection de D. Grenier 20ᵉ. Paquet Nᵒ 1."

2. For introductions to the medieval art of preaching, see Marianne G. Briscoe and Barbara H. Jaye, *Artes Praedicandi, Artes Orandi* (Turnhout, 1991); also Jean Longère, *La prédication médiévale* (Paris, 1983).

3. On vernacular sermons intended mainly for silent reading, see Michel Zink, *La prédication en langue romane avant 1300* (Paris, 1976), 48–65. Zink's subject, defined by the title, is some seven hundred sermons. The surviving sermons in Latin number in the tens of thousands.

4. On whether the text was "upstream" of the putative event or "downsteam," see ibid., 204–10. For a more general discussion see the essays in *Medieval Sermons and Society: Cloister, City, University,* ed. Jacqueline Hamesse et al. (Louvain-la-Neuve, 1998). Leo Carruthers, "'Know Thyself': Criticism, Reform, and the Audience of *Jacob's Well,* in *Medieval Sermons,* 219–49, addresses the difficulties associated with the questions, when, why, by whom, for whom? On the possibility that our piece may be the transcript of a performance rather than a preliminary text, see Phyllis B. Roberts, "Preaching in and around the Medieval City," in *Medieval Sermons,* 151–64, esp. 155, for the case of Master Foulques, a former priest at Neuilly who learned the métier of the preacher by transcribing the sermons of Peter the Chanter on wax tablets. Joseph Dahmus, "Fifth-Century Monastic Wine in a Fifteenth-Century Bottle," in *Medieval Sermons,* 241–59, illustrates a situation where sermons delivered in Nuremberg by the Dominican Johannes Niedler were so popular that he was asked by the honorable women of the city to write them down in the vernacular. See also Louis-Jean Bataillon, ed., *La prédication au XIIIᵉ siècle en France et Italie* (Aldershot, Hants, 1993), esp. "Approaches to the Study of Medieval Sermons," 19–35.

5. Albert Lecoy de la Marche, *La chaire française au moyen âge* (Geneva, 1974),185–89; Zink, *Prédication,* 43–46 and 240–43. Both au-

thors were utterly seduced by the power of this sermon, and both return repeatedly to the piece, quoting substantial portions of the text. Zink considered it one of the only truly "successful" sermons he had studied.

6. For the chronology of construction at Amiens Cathedral, see Stephen Murray, *Notre-Dame, Cathedral of Amiens: The Power of Change in Gothic* (Cambridge, UK, 1996). The funds for constructing a Gothic cathedral in the thirteenth century would have come mostly from the regular income of the clergy. In this case, the clergy owned a great deal of land around Amiens and held commercial rights in the city, including a share of the profits from city ports and tolls on navigation on the Somme River. Contributions from the village folk of the diocese could also provide a substantial income. Such contributions provided the largest single item of receipt in the earliest surviving building accounts of Troyes Cathedral (1290s); see Stephen Murray, *Building Troyes Cathedral: The Late Gothic Campaigns* (Bloomington, 1987).

7. Johann Baptist Schneyer, *Repertorium des lateinischen Sermones des Mittelalters für die Zeit 1150–1350,* 9 vols. (Münster, 1969–80), esp. 3:510–66.

8. On affective response in relation to sermons, see Nicole Bériou, "De la lecture aux épousailles: Le rôle des images dans la communication de la Parole de Dieu au XIIIᵉ siècle," *Cristianesimo nella storia* 14 (1993): 535–68.

9. Estimates on the date of the Amiens choir screen, demolished between 1751 and 1755, range from the 1260s to around 1300. See Françoise Baron, "Mort et résurrection du jubé de la cathédrale d'Amiens," *Revue de l'art* 87 (1990): 29–41; Charles Little, "Monumental Sculpture from Amiens in American Collections," *Pierre, lumière, couleur: Etudes d'histoire de l'art du moyen âge en l'honneur d'Anne Prache* (Paris, 1999), 243–53. Audiences gathered in front of the arcaded ensemble would have viewed twelve brightly painted sculptured Passion scenes, from the entry into Jerusalem to the descent into limbo. In the center, directly above the arched opening to the choir, were images of the Last Judgment capped with a sumptuous panel depicting the Virgin and Child

surmounted by a crucifix flanked by Mary and John. The images of Christ's suffering certainly resonate with the preacher's descriptions of the torments inflicted on Christ as a result of man's sins. These potential linkages are to be treated with some caution, however, since the screen may be later than the sermon, which, as we shall see, was not intended principally for delivery in the cathedral.

10. Lecoy de la Marche, *Chaire française,* 187: "Son discours est écrit à la hâte et ne semble qu'un premier jet: les répétitions abondent, l'enchaînement est presque nul. L'éloquence élevée fait défaut; mais que de mouvement, que de naturel, que d'imprévu dans les digressions, que de charme dans le long récit de l'anecdote finale!" (See also ibid., 413–16, where Lecoy de la Marche quotes the last part of the sermon, the story of the merchant who lost his gold, and concludes that "il n'y a point d'aussi joli trait dans toute l'antiquité.") However, the text seems too neatly written to be a preliminary draft. That it may have served for the purposes of silent reading is suggested by headings that were inserted later: *De Magdalene, De scriptis sancti Geronimi, De Theophili, De sancto Mattheo.* As Zink suggests, these headings might have allowed the text to find its place in a collection of saints lives or exempla *La prédication,* 206).

11. Murray, *Notre-Dame,* chap. 8, "The Portals: Access to Redemption," 103–23.

12. Lawrence Duggan, "Was Art Really the 'Book of the Illiterate'?" *Word and Image* 5 (1989): 227–51, emphasizes the need for verbal mediation in the comprehension of medieval art. Beyond mediating the encounter with the sculptural program, sermons might be considered more powerful than the sacraments in opening the door of salvation. See Nicole Bériou, *La prédication de Ranulphe de la Houblonnière: Sermons aux clercs et aux simples gens à Paris aux XIII^e siècle* (Paris, 1987), 96, quoting Humbert de Romans: "Salvation is available through the sacraments, but preaching is even more effective since it moves people's hearts and prepares them, whereas the sacraments can only assure the salvation of those whose hearts are already prepared to receive them" (translation mine).

13. John Ruskin, "The Bible of Amiens," in *Our Fathers Have Told Us: Sketches in the History of Christendom for Boys and Girls Who Have Been Held at Its Fonts* (Orpington, 1884), published in *Collected Works,* vol. 33 (London, 1908); Marcel Proust, Preface to *La Bible d'Amiens par John Ruskin* (Paris, 1986).

14. Pierre Feret, *La faculté de théologie de Paris et ses docteurs les plus célèbres: Moyen âge et époque moderne* (Paris, 1896), 231.

15. The sermon was published by A. Crampon, "Un sermon prêché dans la cathédrale d'Amiens vers l'an 1260," *Mémoires de la Société des Antiquaires de Picardie* 25 (1876): 550–601. Crampon's text is compromised, however, by errors and omissions, and it is inaccessible to wider audiences. Just as a preacher in his *protheme* might apologize for his unworthiness in relation to the task at hand, I need to point out that I am an art historian, not a historian of literature, and I make no pretense at a critical edition.

## CHAPTER 1

1. The commandment that feast days be respected goes back to Moses; see Leviticus 23.

2. Georges Durand, *Monographie de l'église Notre-Dame, cathédrale d'Amiens,* 3 vols. (Paris, 1901–3), esp. 1:34. It should be remembered that a cathedral was not just an urban church, but that it served the rural folk of an entire diocese. Given the intense competition for urban resources, the cathedral clergy might, at times, be at odds with the *bourgeois.* The rural folk of the surrounding villages, many of whom could see the Gothic cathedral across the Picard plain, could generally be counted on for support.

3. Murray, *Notre-Dame,* 62.

4. Zink, *Prédication,* 74, 205.

5. Larissa Taylor has similarly argued for consideration of the entire sermon, not just the predictable rehearsal of the preacher's invocation of the terrors of death and hell. See "God of Judgement, God of

Love: Catholic Preaching in France, 1460–1560," *Historical Reflections/ Reflections Historiques* 26 (2000): 247–68.

## CHAPTER 2

1. Zink's identification of the halfway point is based on the assumption, probably correct, that the missing conclusion of the sermon amounted to one page. He lays out a symmetrical structure of six sections, organized in two groups of three (like a Gothic traceried window; *Prédication,* 241–42). The following provides an abbreviated synopsis. Part I establishes and defines the relationship between the audience and the church:

1. Invitation to come to church and condemnation of those who have not.
2. Invitation to seek a good ending in life with the help of Mary; for example, the clerk Theophilus. To achieve this good ending, you need God's forgiveness, received through confession and indulgences.
3. Theoretical justification of the sale of indulgences.

Part II invokes the gifts of the bishop to those who help and donate to the church:

1. Enumeration of the considerable value of indulgences in alleviating the sufferings of purgatory; gains to be enjoyed by ancestors who are already in purgatory.
2. The power of the perpetual prayers of diocesan clergy.
3. Absolutions from ill-founded oaths and unkept promises.

2. Interestingly, the preacher anticipates this thought in his treatment of those who followed Christ—different people did so for different reasons.

3. Larissa Taylor, *Soldiers of Christ* (New York, 1992), 86. This balanced view of the mechanism of preaching is also present in Taylor's "God of Judgement, God of Love."

4. On liturgical cursing, see Lester Little, *Benedictine Maledictions: Liturgical Cursing in Romanesque France* (Ithaca, 1993). It is interesting that Last Judgment tympana originated in the period and area (especially northeast France and beyond) that Little writes about.

5. The phrasing is reminiscent of Richard de Fournival; see Jeanette Beer, trans., *Master Richard's Love Bestiary and Response* (Berkeley and Los Angeles, 1986).

6. Katherine Ludwig Jansen, *The Making of the Magdalen* (Princeton, 2000), examines the importance of Mary Magdalene in sermons of the thirteenth and fourteenth centuries. See especially 270–77, on the *Apostola Apostolorum.*

7. Theophilus is nowhere to be found in the sculpture of the Amiens portals. Neither is Saint Martin, although Christ's apparition to him in the form of a beggar was said to have taken place near the site of the cathedral in 337. Saint John the Baptist, whose head was enshrined in an upstairs chamber tacked on the south flank of the choir, is also absent from the portals.

8. We should not forget that the admonition against taking the name of God in vain is the first commandment. Sacrilegious oaths are everywhere apparent in Chaucer's *Canterbury Tales,* whose characters employ many of the same oaths as those found here.

9. The story of the return of wealth that had been lost or stolen was common in medieval art and literature. One example is the Saint Nicholas window at Auxerre (Wolfgang Kemp, *The Narratives of Gothic Stained Glass* [Cambridge, 1997], 28–29). And, of course, in Chaucer's "Pardoner's Tale" the discovery of great wealth is associated with a bad ending.

10. It is worth noting, however, that our sermon presents no negative stereotype of merchants as a group—a strategy that, one imagines, might have piqued the interest of hard-working rural people skeptical

about wealth not generated from the products of the land. Carruthers, "Know Thyself," 225, comments on the dishonesty of merchants as a choice target of preachers.

## CHAPTER 3

1. "Par doner a on pardon" (103). There are other situations in which the use of a particular word with a double meaning could have caught the attention of the audience—for instance, the word *pis* (185), which can mean "chest" *(poitrine)* or "piss"; and *nés* (183), which could convey "nose" or "denial."

2. There was, of course, a common stock of rhetorical strategies for sermons to the lay folk. Audiences may have developed some degree of immunity to the preacher's tricks.

3. *Bele(s) douce gent,* 39 times; *biaus amis et tu bele amie,* 4 times; *bele(s) gent,* twice; *biaus amis,* once; *dame,* once; *mi ami, mes amies, mi fil, mes files,* once.

4. Our preacher's means of addressing his audience and his specific attention directed to a woman were not unusual; see Lecoy de la Marche, *Chaire française,* 209; Carruthers, "Know Thyself," 224, and Zink, *Prédication,* 159.

5. Siegfried Wenzel, *Macaronic Sermons: Bilingualism and Preaching in Late-Medieval England* (Ann Arbor, 1994). The term, coined in the 1490s, originally referred to poetry characterized by a mixture of Latin hexameters with vernacular words and expressions. *Macarones* were made from a dough of flour, cheese, and butter. The word conveys something rustic and coarse—a bit like *Gothic.*

6. Geoffrey Chaucer, *The Canterbury Tales,* translated into modern English by Nevill Coghill (Harmondsworth, 1951; repr. 1977), 241.

7. On the subject of parody in sermons, see Sander L. Gilman, *The Parodic Sermon in European Perspective* (Wiesbaden, 1974). Gilman provides the widest definition of parody as "a literary form which is created by incorporating elements of an already existing form in a manner creating a conscious contrast." Compare this with Auerbach's *sermo*

*humilis*. Gilman tends to concentrate on more obviously subversive sermons associated with the Feast of Fools and with the period of the Reformation. Although the subversion inherent in our piece is somewhat more subtle, many of Gilman's insights still apply—particularly his treatment of Latin fragments, partly unintelligible to the audience, as projecting a kind of magic power (22).

8. Jacques de Vitry urged his congregation not to swear oaths except for the purpose of making peace, "nec sacramenta iurentur nisi pro pace facienda," see Carolyn A. Muessig, "Audience and Sources in Jacques de Vitry's 'Sermones feriales et communes,'" in *Medieval Sermons*, 186.

9. The problem of engaging the attention of the audience has been addressed by many of the secondary sources on preaching; see, for example, Carruthers, "Know Thyself," 219–40, esp. 221.

10. For the community of the deceased present at the mass, see John Bossy, "The Mass as a Social Institution, 1220–1700," *Past and Present* 100 (1983): 29–61.

11. Erich Auerbach, *Mimesis: The Representation of Reality in Western Literature,* trans. Willard R. Trask (Princeton, 1968), esp. 24–49, where the author contrasts the prose of Petronius and Tacitus with the account of Peter's denial of Christ in Mark's Gospel. The classical tradition depended on fully externalized descriptions, with the personae cast in uniform light, their physical characteristics clearly delineated. The new tradition depended on a contrast between parts of the narrative that were brought into high relief while other parts remained obscure. It focused on tension and forward movement, the problematic and the process of becoming, and sought the typological linkages between multiple narratives.

12. Kemp, *Gothic Stained Glass* (Cambridge, 1997).


CHAPTER 4

1. The present study does not attempt a traditional art historical description and historiographical account of the portals of Amiens Cathedral. For an overview of the problem, see Murray, *Notre-Dame,*

103–27; for a virtual reality exploration, see www.learn.columbia.edu/ Mcahweb/Amiens.html.

2. As I began to write this book, the cleaning the west facade sculpture was still underway; that work has since been finished. The process of cleaning has simply created another set of problems as we debate what to do with the surviving flecks of paint that form a strange camouflage on the surface of some of the figures. Should the paint be restored or the figures left in their mottled state?

3. An extreme example of such cataloging and division into "hands" in regard to Amiens is the work of Wolfgang Medding, *Die Westportale der Kathedrale von Amiens und ihre Meister* (Augsburg, 1930).

4. Duggan, "Was Art Really the 'Book of the Illiterate'?"

5. Aron Gurevich demonstrates an approach that links oral communication with image in his *Medieval Popular Culture: Problems of Belief and Perception,* trans. János M. Bak and Paul A. Hollingsworth (Cambridge, 1988); for example, 145: "One should also consider that the scenes represented in the 'Bible in stone' on church portals and capitals were 'read' by parishioners synchronically rather than diachronically. Visual art tends to orientate the viewer toward joining various scenes into a simultaneous picture."

6. Kemp, *Gothic Stained Glass.*

7. I believe that we can identify this learned program with the agency of the distinguished theologian who was dean of the chapter when work began on the Gothic cathedral, namely Jean d'Abbeville; see Murray, *Notre-Dame,* 120–23.

8. Adolph Katzenellenbogen considered that the prophets to our right offered consolation and those to our left admonition; see "The Prophets on the West Façade of Amiens Cathedral," *Gazette des Beaux Arts,* ser. 6, 40 (1952): 241–60.

9. A short text may have been painted on the banderole carried by each prophet.

10. The idea of the apostles as humans who had constructed themselves in the image of Christ and as models for the Christian life is ex-

pressed most cogently by Marie-Humbert Vicaire, *L'imitation des apôtres: moines, chanoines, mendiants, IVᵉ–XIIIᵉ siècles* (Paris, 1963).

11. The correction of the audience through visual images is a theme explored by Edward C. Rouse in the context of English late medieval wall painting: "Wall Paintings in the Church of St. John the Evangelist, Corby, Lincolnshire," *Archaeological Journal* 100 (1943): 150–76. I am grateful to Jennie Edes-Pierotti for this citation.

12. For the sermon's portrayal of Christ the Judge, see 148; for the continuing sufferings of Christ, see 175–77 and 188–97.

13. Paul said, "Be ye followers of me, as I also am of Christ" (1 Corinthians 4:16, 11:1). See Vicaire, *Imitation,* 10.

14. The figure wears a cowled habit and covers his hands.

15. Wilhelm Schlink, *Der Beau-Dieu von Amiens: Das Christusbild der gotischen Kathedrale* (Frankfurt am Main, 1991), points not only to multiple images of Christ in the portal but also to multiple images of the Virgin Mary, who is the fulcrum of the sermon.

16. Of course, this is an illusion, since the figures are freestanding.

17. The educated, down to the connoisseurs of our day, have often found the sculpture "of poor quality," failing to recognize the tropological intent.

18. Originally the episcopal tombs in the nave of the cathedral were placed in the center nave, directly behind the image of Christ on the trumeau of the central portal. The bronze effigies show the bishops, clearly types of Christ, trampling beasts and bestowing blessings. Even the sculptural technique evokes a spiritual trope: molten bronze poured into a mold forms the images just as Christ forms the obedient Christian.

19. Gurevich, *Medieval Popular Culture,* 49–54.

20. *Acta Sanctorum,* Septembris, part 7 (Antwerp, 1760), p. 34; translation mine.

21. A procession to the Tower of Jerusalem, to the southeast of the cathedral, was part of the Easter liturgy at Amiens; see Baron, "Mort et résurrection," 33.

22. The statue representing the saint may have originally been carved

as the Virgin Mary and put aside, to be reemployed later as a virgin prototype; see Murray, *Notre-Dame,* chap. 8. On the saints of Amiens, see Jules Corblet, *Hagiographie du diocèse d'Amiens,* 5 vols. (Amiens, 1868–75).

23. These figures carry banderoles, as the prophets do; they may have been carved as prophets but deployed as saints.

24. The linked *sponsus* and *sponsa* of the tympanum refer to the Song of Songs, a favorite theme in the sermons of Jean d'Abbeville, who was dean of the Amiens chapter at the time work on the Gothic cathedral began. The Song provided the perfect image of the union of the soul with God. In relation to this image William of Saint-Thierry wrote, "Lord our God, you have created us in your image and resemblance so that we can contemplate you and rejoice in you. We can only contemplate you and rejoice in you inasmuch as we become like you" (*Commentaire sur le Cantique des cantiques,* ed. and trans. Marie-Madeleine Davy [Paris, 1958], 33; English translation mine). On the invention of the central image of the linked *sponsus* and *sponsa,* see Marie-Louise Thérel, *Le triomphe de la Vierge-Eglise: à l'origine du décor du portail occidental de Notre-Dame de Senlis* (Paris, 1984).

25. Marcia R. Rickard, "The Iconography of the Virgin Portal at Amiens," *Gesta* 22 (1983): 147–57.

26. The story of the lantern comes from P. Janelle, "Le voyage de Martin Bucer et Paul Fagius en Angleterre en 1549," *Revue d'histoire et de philosophie religieuses,* 1928, 162–77. Recent cleaning of the cathedral has revealed more than twenty-six coats of paint on this statue, which attests to its continued power as an object of physical devotion.

## CONCLUSION

1. This campaign included an enhanced emphasis on penance and confession as well as on preaching, catechism, instruction in the lives of the saints, and the figurative programs of sculpture and stained glass. The objective of the campaign, which had its roots in Gregorian reform, was nothing less than a completely new kind of sanctity. In the early

Middle Ages, personal sanctity was set apart from the lives of ordinary people; it remained the privilege of monks. Inspired by the image of the apostolic church, the Gregorian movement called on all Christians to come to sanctity. The clergy was charged to lead everybody, lay folk as well as clerics, to heaven. Vicaire (*Imitation,* 62–63) describes this transition in words remarkably similar to those of our preacher (3 and 134). The program culminated with the mission of the mendicants, a fact that may be reflected in the portrayal of Saint Francis leading the elect to heaven in the tympanum of the central portal at Amiens. This image, datable to the years around 1235–40, is perhaps the first sculptured image of Saint Francis in the north.

2. Of particular importance in this regard is Gurevich, *Medieval Popular Culture,* esp. 35. Citing Bakhtin, he identifies a third party in any communication, the "superaddressee," who stands above both participants (here, preacher and congregation). As the "superaddressee," we face the task of unscrambling the "real."

3. Robert Fossier, *La terre et les hommes en Picardie jusqu'à la fin du XIIIᵉ siècle,* 2 vols. (Paris, 1968).

4. Fossier suggests that the release of coinage accumulated from Viking hoards provided an early boost to a currency-based economy in the North (*Terre,* 1: 247).

5. The medieval population of Picardy was more numerous than the population in recent times, according to Fossier (ibid., 276).

6. Werner Rösener, *Peasants in the Middle Ages,* trans. Alexander Stützer (Urbana, Ill., 1992), provides a useful overview of rural society.

7. Fossier, *Terre,* 2:572–98.

8. Ibid., 639–43, reports that Jean Florent held 40 hectares of land near Saint-Omer and enjoyed an annual income of 150 pounds, employing a dozen servants. Such people were more than capable of making significant contributions to the church. Fossier concludes that by the thirteenth century, 12 percent of the peasants in Picardy were beggars or short-term laborers, 33 percent cultivated plots that were too small to sustain adequate life, 36 percent lived just above subsistence level, 16 percent had more than three hectares of land, and 3 percent formed a

relatively wealthy elite. "Often peasants one is in a state of misery, three are hard up, four lead modest but secure lives, and two know abundance" (647; translation mine).

9. For the latter, see Fossier, *Terre,* 1:405.

10. On sermons directed at ordinary folk, see Bériou, *Ranulphe de la Houblonnière.* On the various modes of sermon appropriate for different audiences, see Longère, *Prédication médiévale,* 34. Gurevich notes that "the preacher should use the language of the people to whom he is preaching" (*Medieval Popular Culture,* 4). In a broader sense, we have already located the rhetoric of our sermon within a mode of demotic language known as *sermo humilis.*

11. Kemp, *Gothic Stained Glass,* 102–14, explores the *stylus humilis,* a demotic art conceived self-consciously to lend the stained glass programs of Chartres and other cathedrals appeal in the eyes of ordinary people. Jean de Garlande (d. 1272) wrote, "There were three styles corresponding to the three social positions of men: to the shepherds belongs the humble style, to the peasant the middle and to heroic figures, who are superior to peasants and shepherds, the heroic style" (quoted in Kemp, 102). Kemp's analysis of the role of the church in the troubled society of Chartres allows us to understand that these were pictures made by and for the people.

12. David N. Bell, *The Image and Likeness: The Augustinian Spirituality of William of Saint Thierry,* Cistercian Studies 78 (Kalamazoo, 1984); Robert Javelet, *Image et Ressemblance au XIIᵉ siècle: de Saint Anselme à Alain de Lille,* 2 vols. (Paris, 1967). Dom Odo Brooke (quoted by Bell, 102) wrote of the image as a "dynamic force impelling the soul toward its perfection in the likeness." The same concept might apply to the local use of Christian names; the many Amiénois christened Firmin or Jean-Baptiste would find their prototypes in the stock of relics and images at the cathedral.

13. Joel Kaye, *Economy and Nature in the Fourteenth Century: Money, Market Exchange, and the Emergence of Scientific Thought* (Cambridge, 1998).

14. Jacques Le Goff, *La bourse et la vie: économie et religion au moyen*

*âge* (Paris, 1986), translated by Patricia Ranum with the ominous title of *Your Money or Your Life* (New York, 1988). There is in Le Goff's work an underlying assumption that the advance toward capitalism was somehow progress. The same assumption lies behind the work of Robert Lopez, to whom Le Goff dedicated his book. Lopez ("Economie et architecture médiévales: Cela aurait-il tué ceci?" *Annales: Economies, Sociétés et Civilisations* 8 [1952]: 433–38), disapproved of the useless business of cathedral construction that, he alleged, drained liquid resources that could have further supported industrial production.

15. Le Goff, *Bourse,* 99 (translation mine).

16. Le Goff, *The Birth of Purgatory* (Chicago, 1984), 156, assigns a key role to Peter Comestor, chancellor of Notre-Dame of Paris, as well as Peter the Chanter and Simon of Tournai.

17. A trental involved thirty expiatory masses conducted on thirty consecutive days; see Eamon Duffy, *The Stripping of the Altars: Traditional Religion in England, c. 1400–c. 1580* (New Haven, 1992), 344.

18. Le Goff, *Birth of Purgatory,* 168. Le Goff contrasts this creative intellectual atmosphere, in which it was possible to reach an important new synthesis, with the restrictiveness of the following decades. Gothic architecture, creating a "Fourth Place" (not heaven, hell, or purgatory, but an anticipation of heaven), flourished in the same creative forum.

19. Duffy, *Stripping of the Altars,* sketches a similar framework for a later period: "Late medieval Catholicism exerted an enormously strong, diverse and vigorous hold over the imagination and loyalty of the people up to the very moment of the Reformation" (4).

| | |
|---|---|
| Compositor: | Integrated Composition Systems |
| Text: | 11/15 Granjon |
| Display: | Granjon |
| Printer/Binder: | Edwards Brothers, Inc. |